GREAT WAR BRITAIN
GUILDFORD
Remembering 1914–18

GREAT WAR BRITAIN

GUILDFORD
Remembering 1914–18

DAVID ROSE
IN ASSOCIATION WITH
THE GUILDFORD INSTITUTE

The
History
Press

First published 2014

The History Press
The Mill, Brimscombe Port
Stroud, Gloucestershire, GL5 2QG
www.thehistorypress.co.uk

British Library Cataloguing in Publication Data.
A catalogue record for this book is available from the British Library.

ISBN 978 0 7509 6027 4

Typesetting and origination by The History Press
Printed in Great Britain

CONTENTS

TIMELINE

1914

	28 June
	Assassination of Archduke Franz Ferdinand in Sarajevo
4 August	
Great Britain declares war on Germany	
	5 August
	Soldiers of The Queen's Regiment depart from Guildford railway station
15 August	
Guildford's first recruiting march	
	23 August
	Battle of Tannenberg commences
6 September	
First Battle of the Marne	
	15 October
	Belgian refugees arrive in Guildford
19 October	
First Battle of Ypres	

1915

	25 April
	Allied landing at Gallipoli
7 May	
Germans torpedo and sink the Lusitania	
	11 May
	Blaze destroys part of machine tool makers Drummond Bros' factory
31 May	
First German Zeppelin raid on London	
	13 October
	German Zeppelin drops twelve bombs on St Catherine's, Guildford
20 December	
Allies finish their evacuation of and withdrawal from Gallipoli	

1916

24 January

The British Government introduces conscription

21 February

Battle of Verdun commences

March

Married men from Guildford protest over conscription

Guildford Union Workhouse building becomes a military hospital

31 May

Battle of Jutland

4 June

Brusilov Offensive commences

1 July

First day of the Battle of the Somme with 57,000 British casualties

27 August

Italy declares war on Germany

18 December

Battle of Verdun ends

1917

January

German POWs put to work at Guildford's sewage farm

6 April

The United States declares war on Germany

9 April

Battle of Arras

31 July

Third Battle of Ypres (Passchendaele)

20 August

Third Battle of Verdun

October

Surrey Women's Land Army holds recruiting rally in Guildford

26 October

Second Battle of Passchendaele

20 November

Battle of Cambrai

7 December

USA declares war on Austria-Hungary

1918

26 January

Protest at Guildford Guildhall
over escalating meat shortage

3 March

Russia and the Central Powers
sign the Treaty of Brest-Litovsk

21 March

Second Battle of the Somme

15 July

Second Battle of the Marne

8 August

Battle of Amiens, first stage of
the Hundred Days Offensive

22 September

The Great Allied Balkan victory

27 September

Storming of the Hindenburg Line

21 October

Guildford's 'Feed the Guns'
War Bonds week begins

8 November

Armistice negotiations commence

9 November

Kaiser Wilhelm II abdicates;
Germany is declared a Republic

11 November

Armistice Day, cessation of
hostilities on the Western Front

1919

25 January

Heroes' welcome as first men of
The Queen's Regiment return

ACKNOWLEDGEMENTS

My thanks go to a number of people who have made available source material and images, without whom this book would not have been possible.

They include: the staff and volunteers of the Guildford Institute (manager Trish Noakes, deputy manager Jan Todd, librarian Pam Keen and volunteers Graham Hadley and Chris Fitton) who allowed me access to its unique archives of scrapbooks from the period in question. They include Scrapbooks F and G and the Great War Scrapbook. These priceless books were compiled 100 years ago and contain local newspaper cuttings, pamphlets, leaflets, posters, photographs and so on.

I would also like to thank the former curator of Guildford Museum, Matthew Alexander, for his help and good advice; and Guildford Borough Councillor Terence Patrick, for a useful insight into his grandfather, William Patrick, also a former mayor of Guildford, who worked so tirelessly for the town in many capacities during the First World War.

Thanks also to the curator of the Surrey Infantry Museum at Clandon Park, Ian Chatfield, for details on The Queen's (Royal West Surrey) Regiment and for supplying photos of the 1st Battalion in 1914 and the football from the Battle of the Somme.

My good friend Martin Giles (who served in The Queen's during the 1970s and 80s), for his research on the Parson brothers from St Catherine's Village who both died on the Somme in 1916. I must also thank Martin and Mike Bennett;

the three of us give an illustrated talk on the Zeppelin raid on Guildford in 1915. I also thank fellow local historians Frank Phillipson and Roger Nicholas for their research into Guildford's 'night of terror'.

Thank you to another friend, Sarah Bennett, who has researched and written about the Guildford Division of St John Ambulance, including its work during the First World War; and also Les Knight, a former St John superintendent at Guildford, who has a superb collection of photos of the division.

From postcard collection and dealer Tim Winter of Haslemere, I have purchased a number of cards that have been used in this book. Tim also kindly allowed me to photograph a diary/picture book he has in his collection that was compiled by a nurse at the Red Cross Annexe – a war hospital that occupied the County School for Girls in Farnham Road. A couple of pictures are featured in this book.

The Spike Heritage Centre in Warren Road tells the story of the Guildford Union Workhouse which, during the war, was used as a military hospital. The Charlotteville Jubilee Trust administers the Spike, and my thanks go to its chairman John Redpath and dedicated volunteer Jane Thomson, for useful historical details.

I thank Ian Nicholls and his partner Julie Howarth, and Nigel and Val Crompton, who visited me for an afternoon of great conversation about the First World War. Ian has researched the men from Charlotteville named on the war memorial in Addison Road, and Val has family members of the Newman family named on it. Nigel, meanwhile, is a member of the Western Front Association.

Jim Parker and his family gave me details of two members of the Knight family commemorated on the Burpham war memorial.

Fellow bottle collector and historian John Janaway and I (with others) have, with permission from James Giles, the Natural England ranger for Rodborough Common, been given access to investigate the site of the former Witley Camp, a training centre for thousands of soldiers during the First World War. I salute them for the ongoing days we are spending exploring this site.

Dan James took the aerial photograph of St Martha's church, while John Glanfield's research into the wartime manager of the Chilworth Gunpowder Mills has proved very useful.

Marion May collects period costumes and kindly allowed my daughter to model a wedding dress dating from the time of the First World War, and which is featured in this book.

Some snippets of information came to me 'third hand', so to speak. So may I thank those unknown sources.

Many thanks to my wife Helen for reading the text and making vital comments on it. This book is dedicated to her and our daughter Bryony who, I am pleased to say, is developing a healthy interest in history.

And last but by no means least, to William Oakley, the editor of the *Surrey Advertiser* at the time of the First World War. Like a true local journalist, he must have been known to many Guildfordians at the time. After he retired he wrote the book *Guildford in the Great War* (1934). It is twice the length of this book and worth reading for anyone who wants to learn more in-depth facts about the town between 1914 and 1918. In it he apologises for its lack of photographs (production costs being the reason). I am happy to say that this is not the case here due to modern publishing techniques, courtesy of my publishers, The History Press.

INTRODUCTION

The sound of war can be heard in the strangest of places – even far from where the battles are raging. It was an afternoon two years into the Great War and the officer in charge of the men guarding Chilworth Gunpowder Mills walked up to St Martha's church on the hill nearby. Boughs and bushes covered the church in case the crew of a German Zeppelin recognised it as a landmark while seeking to bomb the works below, where men and women were busily making cordite for the war effort.

The sound of guns firing on the Western Front were heard at St Martha's church.

The officer, writer and naturalist Eric Parker, stood with his back to the south door of the church and to his amazement he could hear the guns firing in France – a distance of perhaps 150 miles 'as the crow flies'. He later wrote that he could clearly hear 'heavy guns, the shaking boom, the rattle of musketry as if we were fighting Germany in the next parish'. It came, he said, in repercussion of sound from the large oak door. He stepped a yard to the side and was in the silence of the Surrey countryside; a yard back to his right and he 'was in France'.

This strange occurrence may have brought the actual sound of war to Guildford, but in another sense it was here all the time – from 4 August 1914 to 11 November 1918. Like every other community in Britain, Guildford felt the effects of the war. Not just because of the 500 or so men from the town who died on active service, but also in how much daily life changed. The home front in Guildford had to get used to: a military presence like it had not witnessed before; fears of German spies in their midst; food shortages that eventually led to rationing; the continued call for men to enlist until it became compulsory in 1916; women taking jobs left vacant by men who had gone to war – such as working on the land and making munitions, or volunteering as nurses and helping at a number of war hospitals in the area.

Councillors and other important people in Guildford worked extremely long hours, sitting on committees and playing their part in formulating plans for the organisation and well-being of the town for the duration of the war. Indeed, the actual horror of warfare came very close on the night of 13 October 1915, when a Zeppelin hovered over the town and dropped twelve bombs across St Catherine's Village, a mile from the town centre.

And when peace came and the men who returned were given heroes' welcomes, it was time to look to the future and to return to some sense of normality. But the past had gone forever. And as war memorials were erected throughout the borough, bearing the names of men who had made the supreme sacrifice, the reality was surely becoming clear: a vastly different era had begun.

1

OUTBREAK OF WAR

Guildfordians celebrate the coronation of George V on 22 June 1911.

At the outbreak of the First World War in 1914, the town of Guildford, like the rest of Britain, had been basking in the often-referred to 'golden afternoon'. That is, a term that has come to signify a time of general prosperity; many people saw improvements in living conditions, welfare and education during the Edwardian period.

Indeed, there was an air of prosperity in Guildford, the county town of Surrey nestling in a gap of the North Downs on the banks of the River Wey. The railway had arrived in 1845, after which the town had grown faster than at any time in its history. In 1914, the population was about 26,000. Today, the population in the 'town' area is approximately 67,000, with 137,000 across the whole borough. During the latter years of the nineteenth century, villas and comfortable homes had been built in streets off London and Epsom Roads. Charlotteville was a community that had emerged at the same time – with a mixture of housing including the town's first council houses, built in 1896. Large houses were being built at St Catherine's and on the south-facing Warwick's Bench, where there was concern at the time that valuable and beautiful countryside was being sacrificed. Some of the houses in streets off Woodbridge Road and close to the railway station were home to the families of railway workers and town centre industries, such as the Friary, Holroyd & Healy's Brewery.

To the north of Guildford, Stoughton was a growing community, but retained much of a village feel, as did Merrow. But Onslow Village, built along the lines of a garden estate, and the council housing development at Westborough, had not even been dreamt of.

Dennis Bros' factory on the corner of Bridge Street and Onslow Street. By the time war broke out, it had already expanded with the building of a much larger factory at Woodbridge.

Many of Guildford's inhabitants were reasonably well off. The town had enjoyed celebrating the coronation of George V in 1911, while events such as the Royal Counties Show that was staged at Stoke Hill in 1912 drew large crowds. Guildford certainly wasn't slumbering in that Edwardian 'golden afternoon'. The motor vehicle manufacturer Dennis Bros was fast expanding, attracting skilled workers who were keen to learn and ply their skills as the firm, run by brothers John and Raymond Dennis, increasingly turned to making the latest in specialist commercial vehicles.

There was a distinct military presence: Stoughton Barracks (opened 1876) was the Depot of The Queen's (Royal West Surrey) Regiment, while the military Drill Hall was close to the town centre in Sandfield Terrace. The giant army camp at Aldershot also had a presence, being not more than 10 miles away. Soldiers practised their manoeuvres on nearby ranges at Bisley and Pirbright. The new-fangled aeroplanes could sometimes be seen in the skies over Guildford, with much experimenting with these flying machines taking place at Farnborough, just over the county border in Hampshire, and in Surrey, at Brooklands racetrack near Weybridge.

One of Dennis Bros' motorcars. It ceased production of these in 1913, concentrating on specialist vehicles such as lorries and fire engines.

Britain's Civilian Rifle Club movement was busy training the next generation of would-be soldiers on how to pull the trigger of a firearm with some accuracy. It had evolved in the wake of the British Army being very much on the receiving end of some sharp shooting by its much smaller civilian enemy during the early stages of the South African Boer War (1899–1902). It was soon realised just how inferior some of Britain's soldiers were when it came to using firearms.

A steady supply of boys jumped at the chance to practise a bit of shooting, often encouraged by an enthusiastic clergyman after Sunday school. The boys used either Lee Metford or Lee Enfield rifles with an invention known as a Morris Tube inserted into the barrel, which enabled them to fire .22 rounds instead of .303. This meant that while still firing a 'real' rifle, the recoil was much less. Rifle ranges were set up across the country, often in disued pits or quarries; the Guildford Rifle Club had its range in the Great Quarry, off the Shalford Road. In 1909 it began

Schoolboys learn how to shoot at the Guildford Rifle Club's range in the Great Quarry, off Shalford Road.

THE BLACKOUT

Britain was plunged into darkness when a blackout was imposed. Streetlamps were turned off, lights were not allowed to shine from buildings and church bells could not be rung after dark, lest they attract and guide enemy aircraft.

a scheme in which boys from local elementary schools were given instruction in using a rifle. The aim was to form a club for the youngsters that would act as a feeder for the Territorial Force.

Under the heading 'The boy behind the gun – teaching the young to shoot at Guildford', the *Surrey Advertiser* reported:

> … about forty boys assembled at the Club's picturesque range at Quarry-hill to receive their initial instruction in the use of the rifle … the budding riflemen were very successful with their first 'shots' and George Davis of Holy Trinity School, made twenty-three points out of a possible thirty-five. The score was obtained without assistance.

Interestingly, the report also noted:

> There was nothing like catching them [the boys] when they were young. They wanted to teach them as boys, so that they would require much less training when they became men of the national army. The time was coming when they would require a much larger national army than they had now, which was shown by events that had taken place on the Continent.

Speeches followed the singing of the national anthem. The head-master of St Nicolas School, Mr. H. Butcher, said that it would make the boys better citizens and one great quality which rifle shooting brought out was concentration, and 'anything that concentrated the boys' attention was of good educational value'. The headmaster of Holy Trinity School, Mr. W.G. Prescott, added that he thought the movement would foster real patriotism in the highest degree and that it would be an incentive to discipline.

Some boys were also members of the Surrey Cadet Force. In May 1910, they gathered at the Drill Hall in Guildford for an inspection by the Secretary of State for War, Richard Haldane, with other dignitaries from Surrey. Cadet forces were seen as very important, as these boys would also later feed into the Territorial Force.

Holy Trinity School pupil R. Davis with his finger on the trigger!

A year later, as part of the celebrations for the coronation of George V, Guildford heartily welcomed a visit of 450 soldiers from Aldershot. The local press reported that the men – representing every unit in the Aldershot command and the various uniforms – made an animated picture as they 'marched into town to the music of the drums of the 1st Irish Guards.'

The soldiers were greeted by the mayor, after which they were invited to play sports and games. 'The men entered heartily into rounders, cricket, football, obstacle, three-legged and team races, while pillow-fighting was always the centre of a merry crowd,' stated the news report, adding: 'The soldiers attended a short evening service at Holy Trinity Church', where 'a plenteous tea followed'.

Hot on the heels of the Aldershot soldiers came an inspection of the Surrey Veteran Reserve in May 1911. It took place in the grounds of Millmead House (today the offices of Guildford Borough Council), and some 2,200 men took part – the majority wearing their medals of past campaigns, with one or two being recipients of the Victoria Cross. Field Marshall Lord Roberts, one of the most successful military commanders of the nineteenth century, led the inspection of the veterans. Members of the public watched the parade from Shalford Meadows and it was certainly another local moral-boosting event of Britain's military might.

Lord Roberts returned to Guildford in May 1914, this time to inspect 800 national reservists who had gathered at Newlands Corner. One local press report began:

> Perhaps the most impressive feature of the camp of the Surrey National Reserve at Newlands Corner for the Whitsun weekend was the type of man found in the ranks of that body. When they marched past Lord Roberts the spectators were unable to restrain a hearty cheer, and certainly the sight of the lines of strong, well-built thoroughly disciplined fellows was one to create the liveliest enthusiasm.

Lord Roberts inspects 800 national reservists at Newlands Corner in May 1914.

Again the public turned out in force to witness the spectacle. The report noted: 'Thousands of people found their way to Newlands Corner on Sunday afternoon from Guildford and the countryside, and on the road sides in the vicinity of the camping

ground there were scores of motor cars and cycles and heaps of the ordinary push bikes.'

This gathering was made possible by the generosity of John St Loe Strachey. He lived at Newlands Corner and was the editor of *The Spectator* magazine from 1887 to 1925, as well as a High Sheriff of Surrey. He was instrumental in the formation of the National Reserve as well as the scheme in Guildford to teach boys how to fire a rifle.

The people of Guildford were certainly preparing and also bracing themselves for war, but still had no idea of how or when it would begin.

During the summer of 1914, most people of Guildford, in common with the majority of Britons, only slowly became aware of the political turmoil that was brewing across Europe, which would lead to the outbreak of the First World War.

On Sunday 28 June, the *Surrey Advertiser* had received a telegram stating that Reuter's news agency had reported that the Archduke Franz Ferdinand of Austria and his wife had been assassinated at Sarajevo in Serbia. Telegrams of important events that were received by the newspaper were usually posted outside their office in Market Street, but this time the editor considered it not worth troubling the people of Guildford with another tragedy that had its origins in Balkan unrest.

The printing press of the *Advertiser* was located in one of a number of small rooms behind the front offices, all linked by a warren of passageways. Along with the editorial team and the printers were the typesetters and compositors, the latter based on the first floor in a room with large windows. This allowed plenty of natural light to flood in to assist them in their work of assembling the small lines of metal type ahead of the pages being printed.

However, it was not long before the words 'peace or war?' were in print locally, as the newspaper's leader column on 25 July made reference to the government's latest conference on the unrest in Ireland. But soon after it was the events in Europe that formed the headlines and filled the columns of the British press as people began to look at the events overseas with increasing trepidation.

Tension mounted further on Saturday, 1 August, when Austria declared war on Serbia. Guildford then received a succession of reports via news agencies that were then posted outside the *Advertiser*'s office. People learned that Russia was mobilising against Austria, and Germany had declared a state of war, presenting

Market Street viewed from North Street. The office and print works of the Surrey Advertiser *was on the left-hand side.*

Russia and France with an ultimatum. There was some relief, however, when it was learned that Italy – a member of the Triple Alliance with Germany and Austria – had decided to remain neutral. Early in the morning on Sunday, 2 August, Germany declared war on Russia. The news that the German forces had been mobilised was followed by the announcement that France had done the same. The crowds came into Guildford to learn of the events as they unfolded. What everyone wanted to known was: would Britain become involved and, if so, when?

Next they learned that in London, the Cabinet was meeting to discuss the events and that Germany had invaded neutral Luxembourg, thus violating the Treaty of London, signed in 1839. Several reports then arrived that were later found to be incorrect. One suggested that fighting had already begun in France, and that 20,000 German soldiers had been repulsed with heavy losses. Newspaper sellers from London arrived on Guildford's streets on the Sunday afternoon crying: 'Great naval battle in the North Sea.' The story was found to be false, at which point the news vendors were rounded up, taken to the police station where they were cautioned and then sent packing. Late on Sunday evening it was officially announced that the British Government had ordered the mobilisation of the Naval Reserve. This was welcome news to many, in so much that Britain was not going to stand aside as events unfolded, but all the same it was a clear indication that the country would be involved if actual fighting broke out.

Monday, 3 August was a bank holiday. The weather wasn't particularly fine – following on from an unsettled July – but the temperature was slightly higher than average. Normally, people would have made the most of a day off with perhaps a walk along the river to St Catherine's, or hiring a rowing boat. The more adventurous would take a cycle ride or go on a hike further out into the countryside, or perhaps board one of the many trains heading for the coast. But on this bank holiday, with it looking more and more likely that Britain would soon be at war, most people stayed at home. Besides, with impending movement of troops and equipment, all railway excursions were cancelled.

Guildford's post office, seen on the left-hand side of this view of North Street from about 1910. Further up on the same side is the County and Borough Halls.

The town centre was the place to be for scores of Guildfordians who were intent on hearing the latest news as soon as possible. It must be remembered that these were the days before wireless and even the BBC! Bulletins were being posted outside the offices of the three local newspapers – the *Surrey Advertiser*, the *Surrey Times* and the *Surrey Weekly Press*.

Further indication of the seriousness of the changing events was postal staff being called in at 4 a.m. to deal with mail in connection with the mobilisation of the Naval Reserve. This was followed by the sight of an armed sentry outside the post office in North Street and another at the telephone exchange in Market Street.

As the situation became graver, the local press began to receive telegrams about the need for censorship in certain areas of its reporting. These 'Parker' telegrams warned against printing (intentionally or otherwise) details of troop movements, sailings of ships and so on, that may have been of use to an enemy.

Military men were certainly on the move. Army reservists began to report at the gates of Stoughton Barracks. Their numbers steadily increased, while at the Guildhall in the High Street there was great excitement with the posting of a royal proclamation calling up all men who were members of the Territorial Force. This news saw even more people flock to the town centre to read the message from King George V.

In the meantime, further false rumours were being circulated. It was said that seven German battleships had been sunk in the North Sea and that Britain had actually declared war on Germany at 2 p.m. on the Bank Holiday Monday. The afternoon and evening of 3 August must have been a very confusing time for people throughout Britain as the dark clouds of war moved ever closer.

A call went out for men to volunteer as special constables, owing to the fact that police reservists had been called up by the military. At the same time, there was a rush on food shops in the town as people unwisely began to panic buy, while at the cattle market in Woodbridge Road, prices of the smaller than usual amount of livestock there rose.

A large crowd had gathered in the centre of Guildford late on Tuesday, 4 August 1914 waiting nervously for an announcement, the outcome of which most, by now, expected. They stood not in front of the Guildhall in the High Street, where election results, royal proclamations and the like were usually read out, but outside the offices of the *Surrey Advertiser* in

As war clouds gathered, army reservists began to report to Stoughton Barracks, depot of The Queen's (Royal West Surrey) Regiment.

SPECIAL CONSTABLES
Several hundred men volunteered as special constables to guard strategic points and to enforce the blackout in Guildford. Some were not well received by members of the public, who thought they were overzealous in their tasks.

Friday, August 7th, 1914.

THE WAR.

SCENES IN GUILDFORD.

GRAND SEND=OFF FOR TROOPS.

The Food Question.

REMARKABLE " SPY " STORIES.

SPECIAL CHURCH SERVICE.

Guildford, in common with the rest of the Empire, followed with keenest attention every development which culminated in the war. Since last week-end, when rumours of war began to be displaced by certainties, every scrap of news which bore on the situation was discussed, and newspaper issues have been seized with the utmost eagerness.

When on Saturday and Sunday declarations of war on the continent became actual facts, and it seemed impossible for Great Britain to keep out of international strife, the excitement became intense.

The calling up of the Naval Reserve tended to increase popular interest, which reached its culminating point, when it was announced that Great Britain and Germany were in a state of war on Tuesday night.

There have been many exciting scenes in the town during the week, consequent on the calling to the colours of the Army reserves and the mobilisation of the Territorials.

Early in the week trains going through the station to Portsmouth were seen to be packed with naval men, and several went from this district. Affecting scenes were witnessed at the station when the gallant tars left their wives or sweethearts to take their place in our first line of defence.

Proclamations followed each other rapidly and were posted at the Town Hall and other public places, and were eagerly scanned by the populace. The town had the appearance of a garrison centre up to the time of the departure of the troops on Wednesday. Hurriedly recalled from their training on Salisbury Plain the local companies of the Territorials arrived

Local traders and others have been called upon to provide the animals, and different firms have supplied motor vehicles for the purpose of the mobilization.

Naturally trade has suffered greatly in all forms of business which are not concerned with the food supply of the people, or the provision of war material.

There were signs in the early part of the week of a panic on the part of many people, who feared there would be a serious shortage of food and excessive prices. Many householders started laying in large stocks of provisions, but fortunately a calmer spirit afterwards prevailed and by yesterday practically normal conditions had been resumed.

TERRITORIALS LEAVE.

SCENES OF GREAT ENTHUSIASM.

It became known on Monday that the Government had issued instructions for the Territorial camps to be broken up, and for the troops to return to their several headquarters.

All day on Tuesday crowds waited at Guildford Railway Station for the return of the local contingent of the 5th battalion of the " Queen's " (Royal West Surrey) Regiment. They had been engaged in a big movement on Salisbury Plain involving heavy marching, and when the order arrived to return they were exceedingly fortunate in getting a comparatively early train to bring them home.

Other battalions were not so happily placed, and we understand that some of the regiments had to wait many hours before they could be transported to their headquarters.

In the early evening of Tuesday the arrival

How the Surrey Weekly Press *reported the outbreak of war and the scenes in Guildford.*

Market Street. The newspaper was set to receive the all-important telegram message – via the Press Association – of the answer to Britain's demand that Germany should respect the neutrality of Belgium in the wake of the impending crisis in Europe.

Britain's ultimatum was timed to expire at midnight in Germany, therefore 11 p.m. here. Just before 11.30 p.m., a report came through stating that Germany had declared war on Britain! This was, of course, an error. It was followed almost immediately by a correction that included the fateful words: 'England has declared war on Germany.'

By the time the Guildhall clock had struck midnight, there were only a few small clusters of people left in the town – everyone else had rushed home with the news, wondering what the next morning would bring.

The weekend's local newspapers were full of stories about the events that had taken place in Guildford over the previous days. It was reported that on the Tuesday (4 August) crowds had waited at Guildford railway station for the return of the 5th Battalion (Territorials) of The Queen's (Royal West Surrey) Regiment, who had been on manoeuvres on Salisbury Plain. When the train arrived at about 9 p.m., loud cheers greeted the soldiers as

Off to war in the rain. This is believed to be men of The Queen's (Royal West Surrey) Regiment, marching into Guildford railway station on Wednesday, 5 August 1914.

they marched through the town to the Drill Hall. The regiment's cyclist contingent and its drum and fife band were at the head of the regiment. The men were allowed home for the night but told to return to the Drill Hall the next day. In pouring rain the crowds again assembled to see the regiment depart in two parties for an unannounced location that was, in fact, near Chatham in Kent.

Of the events on Wednesday, 5 August, a newspaper report stated:

Military wagons were loaded with stores of all kinds, and the Territorials were seen polishing their rifles, and generally putting the finishing touches to their preparations. It was announced that the first contingent would leave Guildford at five o'clock. When the first body left the Drill Hall there was a gathering of several hundred spectators, including many of those who had relatives among the Territorials. Headed by Colonel Broderick, the troops marched through the crowded streets to the station, and after a short delay entrained at a siding on the Farnham Road side. Friends were permitted to say good-byes here, and as the train went through the station a large crowd assembled on the bridge and loudly cheered the departing men. There was even more enthusiasm a couple of hours later when a second and larger contingent left Guildford. An immense gathering was in the vicinity of the station to see them off. They had with them machine guns and several horses, and after they had entrained there was again a scene of wonderful enthusiasm as they started on their journey. Not a few women whose husbands, sons, or sweethearts were in the train wept bitterly.

Men from the Guildford area who were reservists in the Royal Navy were seen departing on trains to Portsmouth. A newspaper report observed: 'Affecting scenes were witnessed at the station when the gallant tars left their wives or sweethearts to take their place in our first line of defence.'

Soon after the army had been mobilised, there came an appeal for horses. Notices were served on people owning animals that they might be required. The owners were instructed to take the horses to the cattle market, where a price of 5*s* was paid for each horse. The response was tremendous and all kinds of breeds were offered. A team of local veterinary surgeons examined the animals to determine whether they were acceptable or not.

Holy Trinity church in the High Street was packed for a special service on 12 August at which prayers were said for peace, for Britain's soldiers and sailors and for the wounded and captives. In his address, the rector, the Reverend E.C. Kirwan, began by saying:

> Never within living memory, I am sure, have we been brought face to face with so great trouble as that which confronts us tonight. We must go back at least one hundred years to the time of the great Napoleonic wars to find any situation in England or Europe comparable to that which faces us today, and in our perplexity and bewilderment we have come tonight into the house of God for guidance and protection.

He then added:

> Remember, that you are making history. Remember that this is a war in which we have nothing to acquire, nothing to avenge. Let us fight without malice and without bitterness. Let us be generous, so that when at last it comes we may make a sure and lasting and honourable peace.

He closed his address with these stirring words:

> It may be that those who come after us, and walk up and down High Street long after we have gone, will look back on these days, and will say: It was then that England at last began to know the real meaning of her greatness: It was then that England began to understand the great work she must do for God among the nations: It was then that England at last learnt to suffer and be strong.

A patriotic picture postcard calling men to join the Territorials.

Soldiers other than those of The Queen's Regiment were also flooding in and out of Guildford at this time. During the middle of August, 3,000 men and 2,000 horses of the 1st London Division Territorial Field Force arrived in Guildford. Following a warm welcome, the men were billeted in a number of buildings including school halls, while the horses went to Stoke Park – then privately owned. On the Monday they departed for Whitmoor, Stringer's and Bullswater Commons, where they camped for about a month.

A local press report described the scene at the Worplesdon commons on one of the Sundays while the soldiers were there:

> There was a continuous stream of residents of Guildford and the neighbourhood to Whitmoor and Stringer's Commons on Sunday, to see the thousands of London Territorial Field Artillery who are encamped there. No one was allowed within the lines, but the wide stretch of open country afforded an excellent view. The afternoon was spent in a variety of ways, and a capital spirit prevailed throughout the camps. The heat was oppressive, and hundreds of soldiers went for a dip in Britton's Pond [now usually spelt Britten's Pond], at one point of which there is a large notice board, with the words, 'No bathing allowed in this pond!' The Guildford Angling Society have given the soldiers permission to fish in the pond.

When the London Territorials departed in early September, crowds came to see them off. The *Surrey Advertiser* reported:

> Guildford was peacefully invaded by troops on Tuesday, and the townspeople extended a right good welcome to the thousands of soldiers of the London Territorials, who passed through en route for a destination in the South. Where they came from does not concern us, and exactly where they were going to is equally a matter of indifference, although it was whispered that many of them were hopeful of getting to the front ere long.

The column took three hours to traverse Guildford streets. It entered at the Stoughton end and went on to Godalming, and all along the route the khaki-clad visitors were cheered and welcomed in the heartiest fashion. There were batteries of quick fires, columns of wicked looking howitzers, great guns each drawn by eight huge draught horses, companies of engineers, Red Cross detachments, and battalions of infantry. Tea, coffee, fruit, cigars and cigarettes were lavishly bestowed on them. Many of the men who passed along Friary Street were noticed smoking fat cigars. The reason for this was that Councillor J.B. Rapkins was in Woodbridge Road giving out fragrant weeds by the hundred. The guns went over the Town Bridge and along Portsmouth Road, while the infantry and Red Cross brigade branched off into High Street and along Quarry Street. They were nearly all singing brightly and cheerily as they swung along at a quick step, many chests bared to the breeze, perspiration streaming from brick-red faces.

During these early days of war, thoughts soon turned to defence measures at home. There was some anxiety as to the safety of railway lines, bridges, telegraph lines and the two tunnels to the south of Guildford station on the London Waterloo to Portsmouth line. There was a real fear among local people that, although no enemy had invaded, there might be German nationals in the vicinity or enemy sympathisers who might try to blow up these important communication routes.

Members of rifle clubs – and even Boy Scouts – soon began guarding railway bridges and tunnels in the Guildford area. Some of the men were armed, which prompted an urgent call going out to members of the public to warn that if they were walking near a guarded position and were challenged, they were to answer immediately in case they were fired upon! A number of prominent local people also took their turn at guard duty. They included none other than the High Sheriff of Surrey, Joe St Loe Stratchey, and the Earls of Clandon and Lovelace (East Horsley).

There was also at this time plenty of talk and alarm about German spies infiltrating the area. A story broke that saboteurs had bombed one of the railway tunnels. This was followed by another story that two men, believed to be spies, had been arrested in St Catherine's Village near the tunnel. However, it didn't take long for the truth to be revealed. Somehow the national press had got wind of the 'bombed tunnel' story and had dispatched two photographers to Guildford to investigate. They were approached when they got off the train at Guildford station and willingly went to the police station. A quick telephone call by the police to London soon confirmed they were, of course, not spies at all, and were free to go.

1914 CHRISTMAS BOXES FOR MEN SERVING OVERSEAS
Princess Mary's 1914 Christmas fund appealed for £100,000 to provide a brass box containing either tobacco or chocolate to be distributed to Allied troops serving overseas. In Guildford a fundraising committee was formed and £172 was raised for the appeal.

Stoughton Barracks: Home of The Queen's Regiment

The origins of The Queen's Regiment goes back to 1661, when Charles II gave orders for the raising of a horse and foot infantry to guard Tangier. In 1876 the regiment transferred to new barracks on a commanding position north of Guildford at Stoughton. It became The Queen's (Royal West Surrey) Regiment in 1881, and until 1959, thousands of local men had their first taste of military life at Stoughton.

At the outbreak of the First World War the 1st Battalion, commanded by Lieutenant Colonel Dawson Warren, had been in training at Rushmoor, near Aldershot. It received instructions to go to Bordon in Hampshire and wait for further orders.

At the same time, men from the Guildford area who were military reservists and who had been called up flocked to Stoughton Barracks. Here they had a medical and, if passed fit, were issued with a uniform and equipment. On 5 August, these reservists left to meet up with the 1st Battalion.

Crowds of people lined the streets outside Stoughton Barracks to give the men a rousing send-off. Led by the band playing the regimental march and other airs, they marched to Guildford railway station.

On 12 August, the 1st Battalion boarded a train at Bordon that took them to Southampton. An officer noted in his diary: 'The greatest secrecy was maintained as to our destination, and even the engine-driver did not know, when leaving Bordon, where we were due to embark.' The destination was Southampton. To ensure the public could not see which troops were being moved by rail, large screens had been erected at the approaches to the docks. The battalion then boarded the ship SS *Braemar Castle*, and set sail later that evening for Le Havre.

Stoughton Barracks – the depot of The Queen's Regiment from 1876 to 1959.

2

PREPARATIONS AT HOME

Soon after the declaration of hostilities, War Secretary Field Marshall Lord Kitchener issued a call for volunteers to increase the size of Britain's army. The Territorial Reserve that had been created in 1908 allowed men to serve in the army part time. It had replaced previous volunteer and militia units, but was not considered appropriate for the war that was unfolding, so in early August 1914 on Kitchener's instruction, a new form of 'short service' was introduced.

Lord Kitchener appeals for men to enlist into the armed forces.

LORD KITCHENER
SAYS:-

'MEN, MATERIALS & MONEY ARE THE IMMEDIATE NECESSITIES. ......

DOES THE CALL OF DUTY FIND NO RESPONSE IN YOU UNTIL REINFORCED — LET US RATHER SAY SUPERSEDED — BY THE CALL OF COMPULSION?'

Lord Kitchener Speaking at Guildhall July 9th 1915

ENLIST TO-DAY.

Volunteering for 'Kitchener's Army' meant that a man would serve for three years or the duration of the war, whichever was longer. He was also part of the regular army. In theory he could choose the regiment he wanted to join, but like soldiers in peacetime he had to be aged between 18 and 45. These soldiers had to pass a medical and had to be taller than 5ft 3in.

Recruitment marches and parades in towns and cities throughout Britain began to take place in a bid to encourage men to join up. News of the British Expeditionary Force's retreat from Mons in late August 1914 – which included the 1st Battalion of The Queen's (Royal West Surrey) Regiment – no doubt played a part in the thousands of men at home answering Kitchener's call.

HARD-WORKING COUNCILLOR
Councillor William Patrick was one of many prominent people busy during the war sitting on a number of important committees. He was also secretary of the Royal Surrey County Hospital, and helped transfer injured troops from the railway station to the hospital at all times of the day and night.

The Mayor of Guildford, G.S. Odling Smee, at the outbreak of the First World War.

The first event in Guildford to promote recruiting was organised by the 6th Battalion National Veteran Reserve, and it took place on Saturday, 15 August. The mayor, Mr G.S. Odling Smee; the town clerk, Mr. A.D. Jenkins and the town crier, Albany Peters, took part, with music by the Stoughton Band. A newspaper report stated: 'Thousands of people lined the roads as the sturdy veterans marched along, and when the procession had finished forty men registered their names. They were asked to think the matter over, and on Monday thirty-two of them again presented themselves and were enrolled.'

At a meeting held at the Guildhall on Monday, 17 August, an executive committee was formed, including the mayor and prominent men of the town to oversee Guildford's recruiting marches. One took place the next day, with the parade assembling at the Guildhall. From the balcony, the town crier read the terms of the proclamation 'Your King and Country Needs You'. The parade then made its way from High Street via the railway station to the cattle market in Woodbridge Road, where it was market day. It again featured the mayor, town clerk, the Stoughton Band, and so on, as well as 100 men who had already been recruited for The Queen's Regiment. At the market the proclamation was read once more, along with other speeches, with the town crier appealing for recruits among the farmers, agricultural workers and dealers at the market.

The civilian Stoughton Band provided music for some of Guildford's recruitment marches and rallies. Pictured with them is Councillor William Patrick, in the light-coloured suit.

It appears that the marches were having the desired effect as men from Guildford and surrounding villages soon began to make their way to Stoughton Barracks to join up. By the end of August, 1,200 had enlisted at the barracks, 350 of them residents of the borough of Guildford. Once they had had their medical, been attested and equipped, they were dispatched in drafts of about 100 at a time to other units. In most cases their departure took the form of a march to the railway station behind the band. Each time this was a stirring sight that led to even more men coming forward offering to 'do their bit'.

At the end of August, local newspapers up and down the country published advertisements that appealed for all kinds of men to enlist in different army units. The government continued to place these advertisements on a regular basis until conscription was

Town crier Albany Peters, who accompanied the mayor and other dignitaries at the head of recruitment marches through Guildford.

introduced in 1916. Regiments and detachments that featured in Guildford's local newspapers were wide ranging, and included the 5th Battalion (Territorial) of The Queen's Regiment, the Royal Garrison Artillery and the Bantam Battalion of the 12th Suffolk Regiment. Advertisements for the latter appeared in the *Surrey Times* in the autumn of 1915 and were aimed at men who were between 5ft and 5ft 2in tall (that is, shorter than the normal 5ft 3in requirements) and with a minimum chest measurement of 33in.

In September 1914, Guildford's Conservative and Unionist MP, Edgar Horne, who lived at Shackleford, paid for a page advertisement in the *Surrey Advertiser* that listed hundreds of names of Guildford men who had already enlisted. The idea was that it would encourage others, who were perhaps somewhat hesitant, to do the same. On 19 September, a two-page advertisement was placed in the *Advertiser* that contained 4,200 names, of which 1,100 were from the borough of Guildford. Members of the local Liberal and Conservative parties compiled the list.

Key people in the Guildford area continued to encourage men to join up, using the columns of the local newspapers to get their message across. The high sheriff called upon all men who were fit and between the ages of 19 and 35 to offer their services, and urged all those who had military training to enlist, as they too would be particularly valuable. He also wrote a letter to local newspapers in Surrey urging editors and proprietors to assist the programme of recruiting. It was, however, a slap in the face for many editors who felt they were already doing as much as they could, and were suffering inconvenience as a number of their employees had already left to join Kitchener's Army!

Guildford's local newspapers published recruiting advertisements like this one for the Royal Garrison Artillery.

Guildford's MP, Edgar Horne, took out a page advertisement in the Surrey Advertiser *that listed the names of hundreds of local men who had enlisted, hoping it would encourage others to do the same.*

Although men departing Guildford was good for king and country, it was not long before further employers began to feel the backlash. Shopkeepers appear to have been hit particularly hard in the early days of the war. Some – having lost key staff – refused to let others enlist, claiming the shortage was putting their businesses at risk. In the main, however, they co-operated by releasing men who were fit and not absolutely indispensable.

Towards the end of 1914, the War Office requested that each parliamentary division in Britain form its own Parliamentary Recruiting Committee, to aid recruitment. In Guildford at the time, the view was generally held that there were few men left who would be prepared to enlist voluntarily. Despite this, the committee was formed and a circular sent out asking men to say whether they were prepared to enlist. It was called the Householders' Return and was not well received or widely filled in and returned. But some of those who did fill it in were soon called up, and made their objections as to its unfairness known.

By the start of 1915, the voluntary system was failing and fewer men than ever were joining up. In February, another great rally was held at the Borough Hall that was in North Street. One of the speakers was the Labour MP for Woolwich, London, and champion of the poor, Will Crooks. A report in the national press stated:

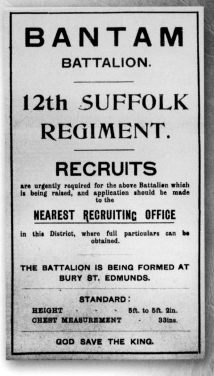

This local press advertisement for enlistment into the 12th Suffolk Regiment was aimed at attracting men who may have thought they were exempt due to their height!

He [Crooks] was in great form on Monday evening. He started off in rare good humour, and kept his listeners laughing for the first few minutes. Then he got to the serious business of the meeting and advanced some cogent recruiting arguments ... To hear him talk of the war and declare that WE SHALL WIN was something to remember. The effect was electrical; each word was shot out in an explosive staccato, the final exclamation being tremendous.

WILL CROOKS AT GUILDFORD.

/ Feb 1915

POWERFUL & WITTY RECRUITING SPEECH.

His Advice: If You Can Go, GO.

ADDRESSES BY MR. W. E. HORNE, M.P., & HON. ARTHUR DAVEY.

Labour MP Will Crooks gave a rousing speech at a recruiting rally in Guildford in February 1915.

The report noted that in terms of recruiting Guildford had 'done uncommonly well', adding: 'Six per cent of the inhabitants of Guildford were in the Army, Navy or Territorial Force, and for a town the size of Guildford that was magnificent.'

In April 1915, a conference was held in Guildford presided over by Major-General Bowles. He was the Chief Inspector for Recruiting in England and Wales. He urged the people of Surrey to spare even more men for the fight, despite key people from Guildford and surrounding districts at the conference making it known that, in their opinion, the whole district had been depleted of eligible men.

To find the extra men needed to fill the ranks, the National Register was introduced in July 1915. Local authorities were instructed to compile a census of every man and woman in their area between the ages of 15 and 65 who were not in the forces. It recorded people's permanent address, the type of work they were in, whether they were skilled in any other type of profession and whether they would consider doing that work, if required. Failure to fill in the form or to do so incorrectly resulted in a £5 fine. The pink forms were sent out on 9 August and collected just over a week later, at which point certificates were issued to all who had completed the form. Across the UK it was found that there were almost 5 million men of military age not in the armed forces. Of those, more than 1.5 million were in a highly skilled job or in employment of high importance and there-fore 'protected'.

YMCA HUT FOR SOLDIERS

With some 6,000 soldiers being in the Guildford area at any one time, a YMCA hut was provided for their recreation. It was erected on land behind J. Sainsbury's store in the High Street and had a kitchen and seating for 450.

NATIONAL REGISTER

Authority is given to

W. F. A. Elsley

to call upon men who, according to the National Register, are eligible for enlistment.

[signature]

[signature: Derby]

------ Chairman of Committee

October ......th, 1915.

Director of Recruiting.

Certificate issued to Frederick Elsley, librarian at the Guildford Institute, for the National Register that was compiled in August 1915.

The final thrust of the voluntary system coincided with rallies across the country in the autumn of 1915. Guildford held a large rally in Stoke Park along the lines of previous events. Those who made up the parade included a detachment of Inniskilling Fusiliers, who were at the time based in Woking; guards from Chilworth Gunpowder Mills; Boy Scouts; representatives of St John Ambulance; Voluntary Aid Detachments; Royal Grammar School Officers' Training Corps and the band of The Queen's Regiment. Despite all this, and with a crowd of more than 2,000, only a small number pledged their services to king and country.

This was soon followed by a national canvass of all men aged between 18 and 40. Known as the Derby Scheme (officially called the Group Scheme), it was named after Lord Derby, who became the Director General of Recruiting in October 1915. Under the scheme, men could continue to enlist voluntarily or attest with an obligation to go if called up later.

It was also announced that voluntary enlistment would end on 15 December 1915. Those who attested under the Derby Scheme and who were accepted for service and chose to defer it were classified as being in Class A. Men who agreed to immediate service were designated Class B. Class A men were paid a day's army pay for the day they attested and given a grey armband with a red crown to signify they had volunteered. They were transferred into Section B Army Reserve, but returned to their homes and work until called up.

7c

Position of
Married Men Enlisting under
Lord Derby's Scheme.

Important pronouncement by the Prime Minister in the House of Commons, *vide* "Times" of November 3rd, 1915.

" I am told by Lord Derby and others that there is some doubt among married men who are now being asked to enlist whether they may not be called upon to serve, having enlisted, or promised to enlist, while younger and unmarried men are holding back and not doing their duty, Let them disabuse themselves of that idea. So far as I am concerned I should certainly say the obligation of the married man to enlist ought not to be enforced or binding upon him unless and until—I hope by voluntary effort and if not by some other means—the unmarried men are dealt with first."

BIDDLE AND SON, PRINTERS, GUILDFORD.

A leaflet issued in Guildford, explaining the Derby Scheme relating to married men enlisting.

The canvassing for the Derby Scheme in Guildford was conducted during November 1915. Those who went around households gathering the details were, in the main, prominent and well-known men from the town, such as councillors and businessmen. Unsurprisingly, they didn't receive much of a warm welcome as they went from door to door!

There were fears among those who didn't want to sign that they might be in a more perilous position than those who had, and would soon be called without regard to their family status or the work they did. Then there were further concerns by those who had signed that they would have to go before men who were regarded as 'slackers'.

It was a very difficult and worrying time for thousands in the Guildford area. However, an immediate knock-on effect of the Derby Scheme canvass was that in the first week, 400 men joined up at Guildford. The canvass revealed that at the motor vehicle makers Dennis Bros (employed building lorries for the war effort), 350 men attested under the scheme. However, their jobs were too important for them to be called up.

The results of the canvass in the Guildford Parliamentary Division was 3,500, of whom 1,138 were single men, with 2,362 being married. Of those who attested, 1,104 had already enlisted earlier in the year, while 3,925 who were willing to put their name to the list were rejected on medical grounds. A Dr Levick had the job of conducting the medical examinations. The sheer number of men examined in such a short space of time evidently took its toll on him and afterwards he was quoted as saying he hoped not to have to examine 'another man for years'.

The government was not pleased with the overall results of the Derby Scheme, so introduced the Military Services Act on 27 January 1916. Voluntary enlistment stopped and conscription took over. It applied to men aged between 19 and 41 who were resident in Great Britain (excluding Ireland) and who were unmarried or widowed on 2 November 1915. There was no longer a choice of which army service, regiment or unit a man may like to join, although the Royal Navy had priority if he indicated that was his choice.

In Guildford, there were claims that the terms of the Military Services Act was not being followed, as married men were being called up. In March 1916, a large group of married men met at the Borough Hall to protest. They demanded that before married men were conscripted, all the single men working in protected jobs should be 'combed out'. They suggested that those jobs could be taken by married men or by service personnel who had been discharged. Conscription was extended to married men, and the lower age reduced to 18, on 25 May 1916.

Guildford saw more than just an influx of military personnel during the war; in September 1914 it offered refuge for more than 100 people from Belgium who had fled their country when it was overrun by German troops. In total, about 250,000 Belgian refugees came to Britain at that time, with up to 3,000 being housed in Surrey.

Guildford had formed its War Distress Committee, and at its meeting on 8 October 1914, it formed a Belgian Relief Committee. Members included the mayor and clergy from a number of Guildford churches. The committee secured empty houses, appealed for furniture, and asked for residents to offer lodging for the refugees.

On 15 October fifty refugees arrived, most with few belongings or money. The French- and Flemish-speaking rector of St Joseph's Roman Catholic church, Father Higgins, and other members of the committee met the refugees and accompanied them to Wycliffe Hall on Portsmouth Road, where they were given food and drink. The children among them were provided with games to play. Afterwards, they were taken to the various places of accommodation that had been found for them.

Later in the month more refugees arrived and were given a similar welcome and assistance. Following an appeal in the local press, Guildfordians gave generously, with gifts of clothing and money. The appeal asked:

There is a local fund out of which the refugees can be assisted financially, and in

AIR-RAID SHELTERS

There were a number of shops and premises in the town centre with cellars that were made available for public shelters in the event of an air raid. They included the Friary Brewery and the 'crypt' of the Angel Hotel.

this direction further support will be required. A special appeal, however, is made for men's and boys' clothing, such as suits, overcoats, shirts, socks, collars and boots, and women's and children's linen, and woollen underclothing, especially stockings and night dresses. These needs are really urgent, and should be forwarded to Mr W.W. Pimm, or to the Guildhall.

The houses that were loaned for the refugees included Collingwood in Woking Road, Hailey (Waterden Road), Roslin (Jenner Road), Stoke Lodge (London Road), and various smaller houses in the surrounding area that included the gardener's cottage at Piccards Rough in St Catherine's Village.

After they had settled in, children attended local schools and many of the men found work. Entertainment was often provided for them that included a concert to celebrate St Nicholas Day (a notable date in the Belgian calendar) and a New Year's party held at the Borough Hall on 1 January 1915. They were also given free use of the reading room at the Guildford Institute in Ward Street.

In 1915, Princess Clementine of Belgium came to Guildford to visit some of her country's refugees, who stayed in the town.

Princess Clementine of Belgium visited Guildford's refugees at Wycliffe Hall in January 1915. In attendance were members of the relief committee, who were introduced to the royal guest. She spoke to them and expressed her thanks for what they were doing for her fellow countrymen and women. Although she also chatted with several of the refugees, it was noticeable that the princess deliberately ignored those male refugees who were of military age.

In recognition of the assistance given by Guildford to the Belgian refugees, several decorations were presented to those who had done more than any others. A Mrs Nicklin received the Medaille de al Reine Elizabeth and Miss C.E. Lacy the Palmes en or de l'Ordre de la Couronne, while the town clerk, Mr A.D. Jenkins and Father Higgins were presented with the King Albert medal.

As the war escalated, life in Guildford was to change on a scale few could have imagined beforehand. The Defence of the Realm Act (DORA), introduced in August 1914, governed the way people in Britain lived their lives. It contained numerous things that people were no longer permitted to do: no one was allowed to talk about naval or military matters in public places; no one was allowed to spread rumours about military matters; the purchase of binoculars was forbidden; trespass on railway lines or bridges was illegal; it was not allowed to melt down gold or silver; no one was permitted to light bonfires or fireworks; the use of invisible ink when writing letters to be sent abroad was forbidden; the ringing of church bells was not allowed; and the government could take over any land, factory or workshop and could censor newspapers. Under DORA, the government introduced British Summer Time to give more daylight for extra work – especially for those working in agriculture – while other conditions stated that no one was allowed to give bread to

Members of the Ayres family, some of whom were bakers in Guildford. An effect of wartime food shortages was that at Easter between 1916 and 1918, Guildford's bakers made no hot cross buns.

SOME SPADES! SOME MUD! SOME SPUDS (PRAPS)

A light-hearted picture postcard reflects the call for people to grow more produce: in this case, potatoes.

horses or chickens, it was no longer permitted to buy brandy or whisky in a railway refreshment room, pub opening hours were reduced, beer was watered down and buying a round of drinks was prohibited.

Feeding the population of Britain while the war was being waged overseas was an incredibly difficult task. The country relied on imported foodstuff and it was not long before German submarines were targeting ships bound for Britain. By April 1917, such was the rate of losses that it has been said that the UK only had six weeks' supply of food left. The production, distribution and control of food were very important features of life on the home front. The shortages that inevitably came about, and the ingenious ways people adapted as well as the measures introduced to help the situation across Britain, were all prevalent in Guildford from 1914 onwards.

At the beginning of the war, plans were soon being drawn up in Guildford to turn unused land over to the production of crops. The council provided land that it already owned as well as compulsorily taking over other parcels of land that were then offered as allotment gardens for a modest annual rent. By the

49

middle of 1918, some 140 acres were under cultivation by more than 1,700 plot holders. They received assistance from the Surrey War Agricultural Committee, through which they could apply for items such as seed potatoes.

With time at a premium, some allotment growers who were also churchgoers questioned whether it was right to dig and sow on Sundays. An answer came from the Bishop of Winchester, who suggested that if they were 'contributing to the stock of food for the nation, they would be doing good work for the poor, and need not feel false to any principal'. But he added that they should still attend at least one church service on the Sabbath as well.

Despite people growing their own, by about the middle of the war most Guildfordians would have been feeling the effects of the food shortages and the controls that were in place, coupled with the shortage of labour. For example, in April 1916, Guildford's bakers announced that there would be no hot cross buns that Good Friday. Back then, these tasty buns were seen as a treat and, unlike today, were only produced at Easter. It was reported that many a young child was disappointed not only then, but also at Easter in 1917 and 1918.

Not only were people constantly encouraged to grow more produce but, in May 1916, the Surrey War Agricultural Committee began to urge those who kept pigs and poultry on allotments and smallholdings to increase their output. They were also asked to consider rearing calves, goats, sheep, pigeons and rabbits.

GUILDFORD'S NATIONAL KITCHEN

A communal kitchen was established to cook food in bulk so as to save on fuel. It was situated in Ward Street Hall and soon became a popular eatery for good, wholesome food that could be consumed on the premises or taken home.

Further schemes were suggested in a bid to increase food output in the Guildford area. A member of the town's Food Control Committee, a Mr W.T. Elstone, came up with the idea of a rabbit warren, which he said could be situated in Foxenden Quarry, off York Road. He produced statistics claiming that thirty does and ten bucks would multiply to around 4,000 in a year and he presented detailed figures of expenditure and expected profits on selling the rabbits. The plan was passed to the council for consideration, but there was a lack of interest, the finance committee declined to offer a grant and the idea was dropped. However, it did raise the subject of keeping rabbits for food and it is believed that the publicity around the warren idea did result in more people keeping rabbits.

Most British people believed that the country would not be invaded, but the government had plans for such an event taking place and issued orders and directives down to county level across Britain. In Surrey it resulted in the lord lieutenant forming a county committee in December 1914, which drew up plans in the event of a raid on the coast or actual invasion. These plans included transport measures and routes for moving people, livestock and other important goods to designated destinations. Lists were compiled of owners of motor vehicles, livestock, and those who kept forage and provisions in bulk. In the main, these plans were kept secret. In March 1916, however, large signs were erected in Guildford, headed 'Notice to Civil Population in Case of Emergency'.

The signs informed people that careful plans had been made and precautionary measures taken should there be an invasion. If a state of emergency was declared, people were to 'remain quietly at home, and they are hereby informed that in such an event many of the roads will be closed to every kind of traffic'. Those who did not want to remain at home were informed that they should assemble at Stoke Park by the entrance at the lower end of Nightingale Road. Special constables would be waiting to give directions as to which routes they could take. It was stated that transport would, 'as far as possible', be provided for children, the elderly and the sick. Everyone else would have to leave on foot, and would be permitted to carry clothing, boots, blankets, and so on, plus money and food. Furniture and 'articles unnecessary for sustenance' were to be left behind.

Conscientious Objectors

There were a number of Guildford men who did not want to fight in the war. A local branch of the No-Conscription Fellowship was formed by those who believed it wrong to take up arms and that the war was unjust.

Those who refused conscription in Guildford appeared before a local tribunal of aldermen, councillors and an army major; the first taking place in early February 1916. Edwin White was an assistant master at the Royal Grammar School, and he told the tribunal that he was a member of the Society of Friends (Quakers) and could serve his country better than by killing.

Chas Moore, assistant secretary of the Guildford Co-operative Society, informed the tribunal that he was a member of the human race, not of any particular country, and that he would not take a human life to defend his own. His added that if he knew how much of his tax went to the army or the navy he would refuse to pay it.

The next objector was Sidney Turner, who declared that he would leave it up to the tribunal to decide whether he was to take up service, adding Christianity was everything to him, and patriotism meaningless.

Alfred Notley said he could not accept any service under the military machine, which was an organisation for the destruction of human life. When the chairman of the tribunal asked him whether he would rather stand by and watch the Germans kill his countrymen, he replied: 'I am not going to kill.'

A munitions worker at Dennis Bros, Henry Bussey, also objected to military service, but said he would continue the work he was doing, 'because I have no other chance in my trade. I have to do that or starve.'

White, Moore and Notley were granted exemption, while Bussey was refused.

Daddy, what did **YOU** do in the Great War?

Despite posters aimed at making men feel guilty for not enlisting, there were those who had strong reasons for refusing to fight.

3

WORK OF WAR

To perform his tasks, the soldier at the front during the
First World War required a multitude of supplies and equipment,
not to mention the actual weapons of destruction. Throughout
Britain, factories and workshops of all sizes operated around the
clock, producing what was required: from weapons, bullets, high
explosives, military vehicles and aircraft to clothing, foodstuff
and medical supplies.

*Remains of
the Chilworth
Gunpowder Mills.*

Many factories already engaged in producing items for the military increased their workforce for the duration of the war, while scores of firms who had previously made other products switched to manufacturing for the war effort. Guildford played its part, with local manufacturers turning out a range of items that included lorries, high-explosive shells, pumping equipment, machine tools and propellants for weapons.

At Chilworth, 4 miles to the south east of Guildford, gunpowder had been made from the early seventeenth century. A site next to the Tillingbourne stream had developed as new methods of making explosives evolved. The Chilworth Gunpowder Company came into being at the site in 1885, a subsidiary of a German firm that was producing a new propellant for weapons – brown prismatic powder.

The manager of the Chilworth Mills in the years up to and during the war was Captain Tom Tulloch. Before the war he had unrivalled access to Germany's armaments industry and, although for ten years he passed on worrying details of how Germany was amassing weapons and explosives, top brass at the Admiralty and the War Office paid no heed to his warnings.

The information this willing spy gathered was often picked up while dining with high-ranking German military personnel, whose tongues liberally loosened up after a few drinks. In 1904, Tulloch learned that a revolutionary bullet, the *spitzgeschoss*, was being introduced. For six years he urged Britain to follow the German military's adoption of the then-new explosive TNT, but his suggestion was refused, as it was seen to be too expensive to produce even though he provided all the necessary details. In November 1911, he informed the British military that Germany was secretly stockpiling thousands of machine guns – a weapon that the British Army at the time considered unreliable. In fact, Tulloch learned that Germany was making Maxim machine guns and was paying a royalty to Britain's Vickers for doing so. All news of this was being suppressed in Germany. But again, Tulloch was ignored; the British military attaché in Berlin declared that the story must be untrue because he had not heard of it!

Coincidentally, Vickers acquired a 40 per cent interest in the Chilworth Gunpowder Company in 1901, but it was not until 1915 that it became wholly British owned. This coincided with new buildings being erected at Chilworth by the Admiralty in that year to produce cordite, a smokeless propellant. Production was overseen by the company in buildings to the east of the existing works. Nitroglycerine, guncotton and mineral jelly were kneaded together with acetone as a solvent to produce cordite. The resulting paste was formed into cord-like lengths (hence its name) by being pushed through dies of the required diameter.

Production at the works continued non-stop, with shifts starting at 6 a.m. and 6 p.m. Because of the high risk of explosions, workers were searched when they clocked on. They then changed into special clothes devoid of pockets, buttons and trouser turn-ups. Women who were employed in cordite production usually worked the night shift and were paid 4d an hour. Both men and women complained of bad headaches, possibly the result of being exposed to the dangerous chemicals, although there were separate mess rooms for men and women for breaks and to prepare food.

After the war, the demand for cordite and other explosives fell, and on 16 June 1920 employees received a letter informing them that the works was to close. Captain Tom Tulloch, then the managing director, had the job of finally shutting down the Chilworth mills.

Rice Bros was a motor engineering company based in Bridge Street, Guildford. During 1915, it produced 1,000 13in high-explosive shells for the Ministry of Munitions. It was the only firm in Guildford to produce shells for the artillery. About fifty

Motor engineers Rice Bros of Bridge Street, Guildford employed about forty-five women, who produced 1,000 explosive shells.

people were engaged at Rice Bros on the contract; of those, about 90 per cent were women. Rice Bros was also subcontracted by Gillet Stephens & Co. of Great Bookham, and made parts for aircraft. Students at the Guildford Technical Institute in Park Street also manufactured small parts for aeroplanes that were sent to the government's factory at Farnborough.

At its factory at Broadstreet, Rydes Hill, lathes and other machine tools were made by Drummond Bros. Arthur Drummond lived nearby at Wood Street and, in 1896, designed and built his own lathe as he was interested in model engineering. With the help of his brother, Frank, the pair set up production in a small workshop at their home, transferring to a new factory at Broadstreet in 1902.

From the outset of the war, Drummonds supplied the Admiralty, War Office, Mechanical Transport and Royal Flying Corps with machine tools. From 26 July 1915, it came under government control. This meant that it had to take orders direct from the Ministry of Munitions, including the prices it set. Its work was then solely making lathes and associated materials as fast as possible for firms throughout Britain.

Drummonds developed new machinery as the demand for new types of machines to make munitions increased. Work at Rydes Hill went on around the clock, with a peak workforce of 460 men supplemented by thirty-five women who were employed for clerical duties.

Production was halted, however, when a blaze destroyed part of the factory in the early hours of 18 May 1915. The *Surrey Times* reported that on his round at 1 a.m. the factory's night watchman, John Harding, noticed that a fire had broken out in the factory's engine room. The report stated:

The works were constructed of wood and corrugated iron, and covered an area of about one and a half acres, and it can be easily imagined how rapidly such buildings would be prey to a fire once it got hold ... The fire brigade received the call just after one o'clock and turned out with the motor engine in four minutes. On arrival they found the whole place a mass of flames, and the roof falling in.

The report added that there was a tremendous explosion that could be heard as far away as Camberley and that people came hurrying to the scene, thinking that a Zeppelin had dropped a bomb. The explosive was, however, due to a cylinder containing compressed air being blown apart. An extension to the factory and three cottages for workers had just been built, while the fire was in the original part. The firemen concentrated their efforts on preventing the blaze reaching the new buildings, which they did successfully, the fire being put out by 3.30 a.m.

Interviewed by the *Surrey Times* soon after the fire, Arthur Drummond said:

> At the present time we have between 280 and 300 hands engaged on the works, and the whole of them will be paid their full wages on condition that they do not leave the town, and hold themselves ready to return to work immediately they are called upon. We shall arrange for the new power to be installed at the earliest possible moment and the new machinery is already on order. It was ordered by telephone this morning, and I am going to London today to expedite matters. As you know there is considerable difficulty at the present time in not only getting machinery, but in the delivery of it, but being a government department, we can rely on government help in expediting the delivery. Fortunately the machinery that has been destroyed is largely of a class that can be replaced, whereas the machinery that has been saved would have been very difficult to replace. We shall probably put the men on day and night work so as to make up the setback caused by the fire and by that means we hope to be able to fulfill our government contracts completely. It is possible that we shall not drop a single item of our government work.

He added that he did not think the fire was caused by foul play.

By far the biggest employer in Guildford producing munitions during the war was motor manufacturer Dennis Bros. At the height of wartime production, it had 800 employees.

A newspaper photograph showing the damage caused by the blaze at Drummond's factory at Rydes Hill in May 1915. At the time, the firm was busy making machine tools for the war effort.

John Cawsey Dennis was born near Tiverton, Devon, in 1871. He came to Guildford and worked for an ironmonger by the name of Filmer & Mason. In his spare time he assembled a bicycle from parts he'd bought from his employer, which he then sold, and decided he might be able to make a living out of this. In January 1895 he opened a shop, the Universal Athletic Stores, in Guildford High Street. His brother Raymond (born 1878) also moved to Guildford and became a junior partner in the business. In 1898 they produced their first motorised vehicle – a tricycle with a single-cylinder motor. John was caught speeding on it – doing 16mph – and was fined £1. However, he turned the publicity he received from this minor crime to his advantage.

The business was moved to premises in former militia barracks in Friary Street and then in 1901 to a building on the corner of Onslow Street and Bridge Street. Although construction of the building had just started when John and Raymond Dennis purchased it, it is considered to be one of the world's first purpose-built factories for making motor vehicles.

GUILDFORD HOSPITAL SUPPLY DEPOT

In rooms above a shop in the High Street, women volunteered, sewing pyjamas, shirts and slippers, as well as making up consignments of medical equipment, while men made crutches and splints. The Hospital Supply Depot in London dispatched the items, 166,546 in total, to military hospitals.

A view inside Dennis Bros' factory at Woodbridge around the time of the First World War.

Their first car rolled off the production line in 1902 and a break-through in manufacturing came with the firm's invention of its 'worm-drive' rear axle. This improved the reliability of Dennis Bros vehicles over its competitors. Production soon turned to commer-cial vehicles, and business was expanding so rapidly that a brand new factory was soon developed at Woodbridge. The firm began making fire engines in 1908 and ceased car production in 1913, concentrating on specialist vehicles instead. It was therefore ready to supply the War Department with lorries when it came calling.

In fact, even before the war had started, Dennis Bros had submitted its design for 3-ton lorries to the War Department for approval. With some modifications to the design that included changes to the lorry's radiator to enable it to work for long periods without overheating, the company secured the order. Between 1914 and 1918, it made 7,000 of these lorries. Production at first was much less, as the factory's workforce had been depleted due to about 130 men enlisting. The army then took a further forty of Dennis Bros' specialised mechanics.

It was the first war in which motor vehicles played a significant part and the Dennis lorries proved to be tough and reliable. In a letter, a private in the Army Service Corps wrote:

> Well, to let you know how the Dennises are running. To speak the truth I cannot say anything bad about them. Troubles are very few and the back axels are excellent. I have not heard of one going yet. We get fairly big loads and very bad roads to travel on. For miles we get cobbles, and I must say the Dennis is one of the best we have out here.

Lord Kitchener wrote to the directors at Dennis Bros, praising the firm for its war work.

> I wish to impress upon those employed by your company the importance of the government work in which they are engaged. I fully appreciate the efforts the employees are making, and the quality of work turned out. I trust that everything will be done to assist the military authorities by pushing on all orders as rapidly as possible.

Between 1914 and 1918, Dennis Bros made 7,000 of its 3-ton lorries for the War Department.

Dennis Bros became a controlled manufacturer for the Ministry of Munitions in October 1915, and therefore became unable to supply vehicles to any of its other regular suppliers or secure new commercial contracts until after the war. Other products it made for the war effort included pumping equipment for both general duties and to supply drinking water on the battlefield, vehicles to carry generators that powered searchlights, and fire engines for the home front.

With so many young men working under reserved occupation at Dennis, it was inevitable that some would have been harassed by others in the town and asked why they hadn't enlisted in the services. To reduce unwanted criticism, they were issued with badges that read: 'Working on HM Services' inscribed around a Union Flag. The directors also had a dilemma in that there was a lack of accommodation in Guildford for skilled men who were coming to work at Dennis Bros, at that time in partnership with the Coventry-based White and Poppe, which made engines. The council recognised that there was indeed a shortage of housing for what it described as 'the working classes', so in 1916 Dennis Bros built twenty-eight houses for its employees on land it had purchased in Woking Road.

The Royal Surrey County Hospital in Farnham Road, pictured just prior to the First World War. It treated 550 servicemen during the war.

Guildford was one of many towns that provided an astonishing range of medical care to servicemen, at its Royal Surrey County Hospital and at other sites that ranged from the town's workhouse, a school and at country homes. Instrumental in assisting with the transfer of wounded men and the staffing of these hospitals and places of care were a number of local organisations that included the Guildford Division of the Red Cross Society and its Voluntary Aid Detachments (VAD), and Guildford's St John Ambulance Brigade.

A complex system of care for soldiers who became wounded or sick at the front was operated throughout the war. Even those in the trenches on the Western Front, and therefore relatively close to return to Britain for treatment, often had an arduous journey from one medical centre to another before they reached home, referred to as 'Blighty'. For an injured serviceman, it was usually a welcome relief, as he knew he would be spared front-line duties, possibly for good, and that he stood a good chance of survival. At the front, stretcher-bearers brought the injured a short way back to a dressing station, usually inside a building or dugout that offered some

Guildford St John Ambulance volunteers wore khaki uniforms when they assisted in transferring injured troops to and from local hospitals.

63

protection from shellfire. The walking wounded would also go there. First aid was administered and men with minor injuries, such as cuts and bruises, were sent back to their units. Those more badly hurt were assessed and then dispatched to a casualty clearing station a few miles behind the lines. They were transported there, often over difficult terrain, and by various means – by foot, horse-drawn wagon, motor lorry or motor ambulance, or even via a light railway. The casualty clearing stations were either tented or hutted camps and were well equipped, with good medical facilities. From there the injured would either go (usually by rail) to a base hospital. After further assessment, some men would then be sent back to Britain for further medical treatment at a hospital, or to convalesce.

Patients at the military hospital run by the British Red Cross that took over the County School for Girls in Farnham Road.

At the outbreak of war, the management of the Royal Surrey County Hospital in Farnham Road made provision for its Edward ward and an adjoining closed balcony to be used by the War Office. The hospital received its first military patients on 15 October 1914, who arrived at Guildford railway station.

The St John horse-coach and the workhouse ambulance conveyed the wounded men the short distance to the hospital, where a number of local doctors were present waiting to give initial treatment. This procedure was repeated many times and more than 550 servicemen had been treated at the hospital by the end of 1917. For every bed occupied, the War Office paid the hospital 3*s* per day towards the cost of treatment, food and nursing.

The Red Cross Annexe, as it became known, treated 2,730 patients between January 1915 and December 1918.

Opposite the Royal Surrey County Hospital was the then newly built County School for Girls. At the outbreak of war it had not yet been occupied, and the Guildford Education Committee immediately offered it as a war hospital. This was accepted and the Guildford Division of the Red Cross Society agreed to equip and staff the building. An appeal was made for volunteer nurses, clerical staff and others to undertake the catering and laundry, and offers flooded in along with gifts of small items of furniture and linen.

ARTIFICIAL LEGS FOR INJURED SERVICEMEN
Up to forty volunteers worked at a depot in Onslow Street, supplying temporary and artificial legs to servicemen. The Red Cross Society and St John Ambulance ran the scheme.

Working in conjunction with the adjacent Royal Surrey County Hospital, the Red Cross Annexe, as it became known, accepted its first military patients on 12 January 1915, a number of whom were suffering from frostbite. The annexe's commandant was Lady Rowley, the vice president of the Guildford Division of the Red Cross Society. She worked tirelessly in these roles for the duration of war, despite suffering ill health and the loss of two sons – Second Lieutenant C.R. Rowley of the Lancashire Fusiliers, who died in France on 10 July 1916; and Lieutenant R.F. Rowley, Royal Field Artillery, who was killed in France on 21 March 1918. After the war she was made an OBE.

Like the Royal Surrey, the annexe also received 3s per day per bed occupied, while the Lord Lieutenant's Fund also gave money. The hospital closed at the end of 1918, by which time it had treated 2,730 patients. While it was in use as a war hospital, the pupils who had intended to go to school there had their lessons in various large houses in Guildford.

The Royal Army Medical Corps took over the Guildford Union Workhouse and opened its Warren Road Military Hospital there in March 1916. It treated 7,680 patients, including a number of Australian servicemen.

Guildford Military War Hospital.

Also displaced for a large part of the war were the inmates of the Guildford Poor Law Union Institution in Warren Road. In November 1915, the local press reported that the military authorities were planning to take over the whole of the workhouse, and the Board of Guardians was considering how to house the inmates elsewhere. It was hoped that any 'friends of the inmates' would take them in, or at 'houses with many men gone to the front where women would be willing to take someone'. The guardians were concerned that the 'homes should be good ones'. In the event, 163 adult and twenty-eight child pauper inmates, plus ninety-two infirmary patients, were transferred to neighbouring workhouses, including Hambledon (near Godalming), Farnham and Epsom.

Lieutenant Colonel Herbert Powell and his wife Beatrice. They offered their home at Piccards Rough in St Catherine's Village for use as an auxiliary hospital for wounded servicemen.

Under the supervision of temporary Lieutenant Colonel Herbert Powell, Royal Army Medical Corps (RAMC), the Warren Road Military Hospital opened in March 1916. Doctors from Guildford initially formed the medical staff, until a RAMC surgeon and female doctors took over later. It was the largest of Guildford's wartime military hospitals, with 300 beds, later increasing to 480 beds. Eighty nurses attended to the patients, supported by a number of orderlies and clerks, including existing workhouse staff, who retained their civilian status.

From the early part of 1918 it was mostly used to treat cases of malaria, and closed in May 1919, having treated 7,680 patients, a number of Australian servicemen among them.

Lieutenant Colonel Powell lived at Piccards Rough in St Catherine's Village. At the outbreak of the war his wife, Beatrice Powell, had been appointed commandant of a new VAD of the Guildford Division of the Red Cross. In 1915, the Powells gave

WOMEN IN THE WORKPLACE
As Guildford men joined the armed forces, women stepped into the jobs they left behind. They were soon working in shops, then in munitions and on the land, while also being employed as bus conductors, postwomen, at the gas works, and as road sweepers.

their home over for use as an auxiliary hospital, but before their home became Piccards Rough Convalescent Hospital, Mrs Powell and a female friend made a mercy dash to France, offering to care for wounded soldiers lying in Paris hotels that had been turned into war hospitals.

Their journey to Paris in late October 1914 on a crowded ferry and then an extremely slow train was bad enough. When they arrived, the city was in darkness amid fears of air raids. The next morning they learned that most of the wounded soldiers had been evacuated from where they had been staying, and for two weeks Mrs Powell and her companion had little to do. They then headed for Boulogne when they had heard there was a lack of nurses at the war hospitals set up near the British Army's headquarters. She later wrote of her experiences:

> We found ambulances full of wounded and dying. The streets were full of them too, and on the steps of some of the hotels and casinos which had hastily been equipped as hospitals were lying wounded for whom beds had not been found.

The two women presented themselves at a hospital offering to help, but were refused. They later learned that without valid credentials their chances of being taken on were slim, and that they may have been regarded as potential enemy spies. Then, by an amazing stroke of luck, Mrs Powell ran into a relative of her husband's family. The man was a consultant physician attached to the armed forces. A few days later, he found Mrs Powell a job at the casino in Wimereux that had been turned into a hospital. However, she and her companion were also helping out at mission hall in Boulogne, serving tea and snacks to soldiers on leave.

At the hospital she sat talking to patients and writing letters for them. Of her time at this unheated building, she later wrote: 'The poor nurses were almost frozen to death, but I don't think the men felt the cold: I think the awful conditions from which they had come made them thankful to be out of it all, for a time.'

She also noted the sadness and horrors of her time there: 'I was able to give every man a sweet each time, but there were too many to talk to, or to write for.' She recalled the 'joy, and even wonder, in the faces of two very young, terribly wounded German soldiers, when I offered them sweets'. She added that they both died of their wounds. One morning, she discovered a man who had died and whose body remained in a bed in the ward. Only the day before, she had written a letter on his behalf to his wife that began, 'I hope this letter finds you as well as it leaves me at present'.

After three months, and with what she described as mixed feelings, Mrs Powell returned home. But it was not long before her work caring for wounded soldiers was to resume.

The War Office accepted the offer by Herbert and Beatrice Powell of their home as a Red Cross hospital in March 1915. Mrs Powell later wrote:

> We gladly gave consent, little perhaps realising the greatness of the upheaval. We were told that we must provide fifty beds, and this meant storing all the furniture of the sitting rooms and that of the bedrooms except our own and those for the staff ... After the furniture was cleared out the Red Cross equipment arrived, and with it a horde of VADs and their officers, to do the arranging.

The first patients arrived on 11 April 1915, and a little too soon for Mrs Powell, as she noted:

> The telephone rang, and orders came through that we must expect thirty men that evening. I was in despair, Sunday of all days, and very little food in the house and no VADs. I implored the man at the other end of the telephone to let us off till the next day, but of course he couldn't, and it came to me as a shock to realise the inevitability of the whole thing – what it meant to be part of the military machine.

TREATS FOR THE TROOPS
Women and schoolchildren
made up comfort parcels
for men serving overseas.
The donated items were then
dispatched from Stoughton
Barracks. However, one
set of Christmas parcels
bound for men fighting in
Mesopotamia did not arrive
until April!

Of the VADs who worked at Piccards Rough Hospital, Mrs Powell recalled:

It may be imagined that many of these girls had no knowledge of house or parlour or kitchen work, so I had to do a good deal of training, as well as innumerable jobs not rightly within the province of a commandant. The team was not a very easy one to handle. We housed only about six [VADs], the rest came up for days or part days in rotation.

She also described how the convalescing soldiers came to be at the hospital:

We didn't have men straight from the various fronts because we had no operating theatre … with us, in the real country the men should have had as good a time as possible under the circumstances; and while they were really ill, or incapacitated by reasons of their wounds, they did appreciate the quiet and the fact that in good weather they lived out of doors.

Those soldiers who made good progress in their recovery and were able to walk often made trips to Guildford and back. Mrs Powell wrote:

Everything possible was done for the 'Tommy' to make life a little less hideous (for there was generally the prospect of a return to soldiering) and in the process he was rather spoilt. A bevy of those we had, used to come back to an enormous tea at five saying they had been given already five separate teas, by various kind but misguided ladies who lay in wait for the men in blue!

The Earl and the Countess of Onslow's home at Clandon Park was also converted into a war hospital for injured troops

Wounded soldiers pictured at Clandon Park. It was also converted into a war hospital, treating men directly from the battlefield.

arriving directly from the battlefield. It had a total of 132 beds and admitted 5,059 soldiers. Lord Onslow's dressing room, with its running water and strong north-east light, was chosen as an operating theatre, where 747 operations were performed.

The hospital received its patients from Clandon railway station. Not only did the Guildford Division of St John Ambulance assist with the detraining of the wounded, but two military ambulances with soldier drivers were used, under the supervision of Lady Onslow, who was the hospital's commandant. The hospital staff included trained nurses, VADs nurses and orderlies from St John Ambulance and the Shere and Albury detachment of the Red Cross. The first patients were a convoy of badly wounded Belgians, who arrived at Clandon railway station at 3 a.m. on 14 October 1914. The hospital was kept busy until April 1919, and had two annexes – a house called Heywood in Cobham, and Broom House at West Horsley.

One of the VADs was Margaret E. Van Straubenzee, who was recruited to Clandon Park Hospital in 1916. Writing later of the daily horrors that the staff witnessed, she recalled: 'Several of the wounded had an arm or a leg blown off, and there was one case with both legs and one arm missing. One felt one could not do enough for these poor fellows. Operations were going on day and night.'

DR CECIL P. LANKESTER
Dr Cecil Lankester was busy during the war: he was not only caring for civilians, but he was also duty surgeon at three local war hospitals, surgeon to the Guildford Division of St John Ambulance, and undertook air-raid duties. Commissioned into the Royal Army Medical Corps, he went to France in 1918.

The Guildford Division of St John Ambulance Brigade

Under the command of Divisional Superintendent Martin Williamson, members of the Guildford division of St John Ambulance undertook a wide range of duties throughout the war.

As their needs changed, injured soldiers who had been returned to Britain were being constantly moved from one hospital or institution to another. Staff of the Guildford division assisted in transferring men from ambulance trains to local hospitals throughout Surrey and sometimes beyond. The brigade's horse-drawn ambulance was supplemented by a Napier motor ambulance, while offers from those who owned motor cars to help transport the injured were also taken up.

Some worked as volunteer orderlies in hospitals, while at the Guildford Military Hospital in Warren Road and at Clandon Park Military Hospital they stood in for permanent orderlies at weekends. Others volunteered for night porter work, while all ranks acted as operating theatre orderlies at Thorncombe Hospital in Bramley.

Others sat with patients who required constant sympathetic attention, although for some younger volunteers the experience was often harrowing. By 1917, only members over the age of 30 were considered for night duty at the Royal Surrey County Hospital.

The division's sergeant major, James Lambert, worked extensively at Clandon Park Hospital. He was presented with an autograph book by Belgian soldiers: clear evidence of the efforts he made to make their stay more comfortable.

Many members also enlisted in the Military Home Hospitals Reserve. Working under the control of the Royal Army Medical Corps (RAMC), they took up orderly duties at hospitals across southern England. Members also served with the RAMC abroad at hospitals in France, Egypt, Macedonia, Mesopotamia and India.

Nearly 100 of the 170-strong Guildford division joined the forces, seven of those losing their lives.

The Guildford St John Ambulance Brigade's Napier motor ambulance when new in 1914.

4

NEWS FROM THE FRONT LINE

The Queen's (Royal West Surrey) Regiment fought in many campaigns during the First Word War – from the Western Front and Gallipoli to Mesopotamia and Palestine. Losses were very high – 8,000 men killed from the twenty-five battalions raised. In the 1st Battalion alone, five commanding officers, two majors, sixty-one commanding officers and 1,133 NCOs and men died. Five Victoria Crosses were awarded to men of The Queen's.

The 1st Battalion The Queen's (Royal West Surrey) Regiment on mobilisation at Bordon, Hampshire, in August 1914.

The 1st Battalion went to France in September 1914, joining the British Expeditionary Force. By November its numbers had been decimated, with only thirty-two survivors out of a total of 998 men. It fought at Mons, the Marne and the Aisne, at Ypres, Aubers Ridge, Loos, the Somme, Festubert, the Hindenberg Line,

Bellecourt, Broodseinde, Passchendaele and Arras. At the end of the war there were just seventeen men left from all ranks who had started the campaign in 1914.

The 2nd Battalion was in South Africa when war broke out. It was hurried home and by October was in Flanders, taking part in the First and Second Battle of Ypres, the Battles of Loos, Somme, Arras, the Flanders offensive, and the campaign in Italy. Early in the war this battalion suffered 676 casualties. Men from 'Kitchener's Army', Territorials and later conscripts refilled the ranks.

Of The Queen's Territorial battalions, the 1/4th was sent to India at the start of the war and fought on the North-West Frontier. The 2/4th Battalion fought at Gallipoli and Gaza, reaching Jerusalem in 1917, before being transferred to France. Following service in Britain, the 3/4th Battalion went to France in 1917 and lost half its strength in its first battle. The 1/5th Battalion saw service in India and Mesopotamia, while the 6th Battalion went to France in 1915 and fought on the battlefields at Loos, Arras, Cambrai and the Somme.

By 9 November 1914, when this photograph was taken, the 1st Battalion The Queen's (Royal West Surrey) Regiment had been decimated in battle.

Many of Kitchener's volunteers filled the ranks of The Queen's additional First World War service battalions. They all served on the Western Front. In addition, The Queen's raised labour and young soldiers' battalions, but these did not serve overseas. These were men who worked behind the lines, keeping the military machine moving. They had either specialist technical skills or were unfit for front-line service and were absorbed into the Labour Corps in June 1917.

Whether by choice or what was decided for them, men from Guildford served in a wide range of army regiments, the Royal Navy and the Royal Flying Corps (later renamed the RAF). Their letters and postcards home revealed fascinating details of what life was like: perhaps of a bloody battle they had just been fighting; describing the mud in the trenches; or after their ship had docked at a far-off port and their wonder at exotic sights they could had not have imagined before and which their loved ones would probably never have the opportunity of seeing.

Censorship was in force, with all letters and postcards written by men of lower ranks generally inspected by commanding officers. Any details a soldier wrote that were deemed unsuitable

As this picture postcard depicts, the postal service on the Western Front was very efficient, with letters and postcards soon being received back home and replies and parcels quickly sent back.

Vise Paris N° 831   Reprod interd

YOUR PACKAGE ARRIVED ALL RIGHT A THOUSAND THANKS TO YOU.
Votre colis est arrivé à bon port, merci mille fois.

MILITARY FUNERAL AT GUILDFORD: CORTEGE IN BRIDGE STREET.
Photo by Mr. Harry How.

for reading back home, or information useful to the enemy, were obliterated with an indelible pencil, coloured purple. A postal services section of the Royal Engineers handled the mail on the Western Front. Mail from soldiers to home was delivered free of charge and very quickly too.

Some families who received letters full of interesting stories of heroic courage and near scrapes allowed Guildford's local newspapers to reprint extracts from them. The local press did not have the capacity to send its own reporters overseas to battles, so the letters it published provided a vivid – but possibly much edited – eyewitness account of what was going on.

However, even as the first correspondences written by servicemen were dropping through letterboxes, the dreaded telegrams giving news that a man was reported 'missing' or even worse, had died, were being delivered.

Lieutenant Robert Scott Pringle of The Queen's Regiment is believed to be the first Guildford man to have been killed in the war. He died on 14 September 1914 and he is buried in Moulins New Communal Cemetery in France. He was the son of Mr R. Pringle of Ardmore, Manor Road, Stoughton.

Thousands of people lined the streets of Guildford to watch the funeral cortège of the first two soldiers to die of wounds at the Royal Surrey County Hospital. The picture is a cutting from the Surrey Weekly Press.

WILLIAM HARVEY

William Harvey served as a car driver and despatch rider. He was awarded the Military Medal in 1918. After the war he established Harvey's department store, became a mayor of Guildford and was made an OBE for his scheme to provide work for the unemployed in the 1930s.

Guildford came to a standstill on Tuesday, 20 October 1914, when the bodies of two soldiers who had died of wounds at the Royal Surrey County Hospital were conveyed on 'an open trolley' to Stoke Cemetery in Stoughton Road. The *Surrey Weekly Press* reported: 'Thousands of people lined the route. It was an imposing but respectful tribute to two young men who had done their duty amid a hell of shot and shell.'

The two men were Private J. Hornblow, aged 28, of the Royal West Kent Regiment, and Drummer C. Murray, aged 25, of the King's Own Scottish Borderers. They were accorded full military honours – their coffins were draped in Union flags and a firing party of fourteen soldiers from Stoughton Barracks led the cortège. Several thousand people thronged the entrance to the cemetery, hoping to catch a glimpse of the funeral service.

Private Hornblow and Drummer Murray's headstones in Stoke Cemetery, Guildford.

Those who hoped and believed the war would be over by Christmas 1914 were naturally disappointed. But hope prevailed, and a letter published in the local press in July 1915, written home to Guildford by Rifleman A. Fisher of the 1st King's Royal Rifle Corps, included the following lines:

> I expect you know we are in the hot corner. I mustn't tell you the name. I thought my luck was in when I got away from Mons, but I have been luckier since, having been hit three times by splinters from a shell. We were playing football once and a shell burst between us, so you can guess it has been exciting. I think the war will last a few more months yet, though everybody out here thinks it will finish in August. I think about March myself, unless something unexpected turns up.

In August 1915, Mr and Mrs W. Collier, of 27 Springfield Road, heard the sad news that their eldest son, Quartermaster Sergeant Walter Collier, aged 30, of the 6th East Lancashire Regiment, had been killed in action in the Dardanelles on 9 August. This was their second loss within a few months, as another son – 22-year-old Leslie, a private with the 18th Hussars – had died of wounds in Ypres that February. They later lost a third son, Private A.E. Collier, Royal Fusiliers, who was killed in France in November 1917.

The Gallipoli campaign was widely reported in the local press in 1915, and not just stories of heroic deeds. Newspaper columns were soon filled with long lists of names of men from the 2/4th The Queen's Regiment who been killed, were missing, wounded, had died of wounds, or were sick or wounded in hospital. These lists would continue almost every week until the end of the war. They were particularly extensive in the editions that followed large campaigns, such as the Battle of the Somme in 1916, and the German Offensive in the spring of 1918.

One letter published and written to his father by First-Class Petty Officer Frederick Horstmann of the Armoured Car Brigade spoke of landing at Gallipoli on board the *River Clyde*. He noted:

We landed with the Munsters and the Dublins. We had a pretty hot time of it. One of the shells missed me by about two feet, went through a steam pipe, and out the other side of the ship. After landing we were three weeks in the firing line, and had a rough time, as we could not be relieved. I am writing this in my dug-out, shared with another boy. It's an old Turkish trench, and we have made it very cosy.

Under the heading 'Sniping the Snipers', the local press published a letter written home to his wife by Private H. Spearman, of George Road, from his hospital bed in Malta. He wrote:

I have seen a few hundred of the Turks knocked over, but after one has been into it for about half an hour you don't think anymore of shooting Turks than you do rabbits back home. The best shot I got was about 4 o'clock in the morning. There were several regiments at the foot of the hill resting for a few hours. There were a lot of Turkish snipers in the trees around us, and about every hour one of our boys would get shot. I saw one of the boys get shot in the head. I could see where the shot came from. I went towards this tree and there I saw Mr Turk nicely seated in the branches. I had only one shot, and he tumbled out of his nest like a bird.

GUILDFORD'S TWO VCS

Two men born in Guildford received the highest award for gallantry. Seriously wounded and under fire, Captain Francis Grenfell helped save guns from capture in Belgium in 1914 and was awarded the Victoria Cross. Second Lieutenant Alfred Smith was posthumously awarded his for protecting his men from an exploding grenade at Gallipoli, 1915.

Other letters spoke about women snipers causing 'great trouble'. A Private South wrote: 'The women appear to be between 25 and 30 years of age and the men between 45 and 50. They are all painted green and excellent shots. They either find your heart or your brain.' He added that while he was in the trenches, rations consisted of bully beef, biscuits and 'half a pint of muddy water per man'.

News was also coming through from the Western Front. Battery Sergeant Major H. P. Morris wrote:

You will have heard of our great fight, in which the new Army took part, and were very successful. I can assure you it was terrible – a sight I don't want to see again as long as I am alive. There had been a battle the previous day where we went, and the wounded and killed were terrible to see. They were simply loathsome … in fact, it was impossible to walk without treading upon them. I was taking up a position for the gun and trod on something soft, and it was a body – a German. I covered it up a little as quickly as I possibly could and got away.

Ordinary Seaman Theodore W. Bowler of Guildford died during the Battle of Jutland in 1916 when his ship HMS Black Prince *was sunk with all hands lost.*

'Heroes of the North Sea battle' was the headline in the *Surrey Weekly Press* shortly after the Royal Navy had taken part in the Battle of Jutland against the Imperial German Navy on 31 May and 1 June 1916. Fourteen British and eleven German ships were sunk, with a great loss of life and with both sides claiming victory. Six men from Guildford who lost their lives in the battle are commemorated on the Guildford war memorial in the Castle Grounds. Ordinary Seaman Theodore W. Bowler, aged 26, of Leas Road; Gunner Ernest Holt, of the Royal Marines, of 12 Stoke Grove; and Stoker James Bishop, of Old Farm Road, Guildford, were all on board HMS *Black Prince*. Boy 1st Class Ralph Foxley, aged 17, of Haydon Place; Able Seaman Edward Shearing, of Manor Road; and Ship's Writer Arthur Danise, aged 44, of Stoke Road, were on board HMS *Queen Mary*.

The newspaper mentioned other men who had died and who had either grown up in Guildford or had strong links with the town. They were: Warrant Officer E. Tanner (HMS *Black Prince*), who had lived at 36 Ludlow Road; Sergeant Arthur Sherman (HMS *Invincible*), who had been staying with an aunt in Addison Road while on leave a month previously; and Boy 1st Class Alfred Hoare (HMS *Queen Mary*), aged 16. Originally from Essex, Hoare had worked at the County and Borough Halls in North Street.

Able Seaman Edward Shearing from Guildford was one of the 1,266 officers and men who died when HMS Queen Mary *was sunk during the Battle of Jutland in 1916.*

Other families were relived to hear that their sons had survived the battle. The press reported:

> Mr and Mrs F.A. Hicks, of Roseneath, Woodbridge Road, had a pleasant surprise on Tuesday evening, when their sailor son, Albert, paid an unexpected visit home. Knowing that he was with the Grand Fleet they had naturally been anxious. Albert is only 17 years of age, was engaged in the battle, and rendered a good account of himself.

Stoker William Reeves of 12 New Cross Road was on HMS *Hogue* when it was torpedoed. He was in the sea for three hours before finally being picked up by a Dutch boat, and landed in Holland.

Just over a month later, it was the opening days of another terrible battle that dominated the news. The Battle of the Somme (1 July–18 November 1916) claimed nearly one million men from both sides, either wounded or killed. The first day of the battle was the worst in the history of the British Army with nearly 60,000 casualties alone. The *Surrey Advertiser* reported:

> The nation has been thrilled by the news of the great advance made by the British and French Forces during the past week against the Germans in the Battle of the Somme. We understand at least three battalions of The Queen's were in the advance. Very little definitive news of the actual part they took in the fight has come through, but there seems to be no reason doubting that they were in the thick of it.

Indeed they were, and the newspaper published details of a letter written by a wounded NCO from The Queen's Regiment.

The dawn broke lovely on Saturday morning, the sun shining beautifully. Then at 7.30 exactly our guns started firing farther back. The whistle went and we were out of our trenches and across No Man's Land in a jiffy. A lot of Germans put up their hands and said: 'Mercy, Comrade.' Did we give mercy? Oh! No, they got the bayonet instead. We went through them right and left, turned back and then through them again. If that is Somme battle, I don't want any more of it.

Reports in the following week's edition gave an indication of the reality of what had happened, with headlines proclaiming: 'Ninety officers killed, wounded and missing' and 'Heavy casualties among the NCOs and men', along with long lists of casualties and short biographical details of officers who had died. One of those was Second Lieutenant Reginald Oakley, of the King's Own Yorkshire Light Infantry. He was the son of the *Surrey Advertiser*'s editor, William Oakley. The report stated that Oakley was killed on 1 July, the same day as his friend Second Lieutenant Dandridge, and that he was educated at the Royal Grammar School where he was in the officer training corps. He had joined the 1/5th Battalion of The Queen's Regiment the day after war was declared and proceeded to India in October 1914 with the battalion. A year later, Reginald returned to take up a commission in the King's Own Yorkshire Light Infantry. He made a special application to be sent to the front, and 'went out full of hope and confidence about a month before his death. His frank and sunny disposition made him popular with all.' Before he enlisted, he was a journalist with the *Surrey Advertiser*.

Eleven months later it was the turn of the editor of the *Surrey Times*, Mr. T.H. White, to grieve when his younger son, Lance Corporal

Lieutenant Reginald Oakley of The King's Own Yorkshire Light Infantry died on the first day of the Battle of the Somme, 1 July 1916. He was educated at Guildford's Royal Grammar School.

One of the four footballs kicked by men of the East Surrey Regiment across no-man's-land on the first day of the Battle of the Somme can be seen at the Surrey Infantry Museum at Clandon Park.

Cecil White, London Regiment, was killed. A letter from his commanding officer to the parents read: 'Your son was commander of the bombing section of my platoon, and was killed by a shell whilst leading his section in the attack on June 7th.' Another letter received from a comrade stated that White had died instantly and the day before had been in 'the best of spirits'.

In mid-July 1916, the *Surrey Advertiser* reported an early version of what has become a famous story of the Battle of the Somme. On the first day of the battle, men of the East Surrey Regiment kicked footballs as they made their way across no-man's-land to the German front line. It read:

> Was there anything ever like it? Men playing a game against death! The officer who provided the four footballs was Captain Wilfred P. Nevill, and was related to Mr Ralph Nevill, of Guildford. The gallant officer – he was only twenty-two – was killed early, but two of the footballs reached the German trenches, and were subsequently recovered. One was yesterday handed into the keeping of Colonel Treeby at the depot of the East Surrey Regiment, and will be among the most cherished relics of the war.

How true those words were, as one of those very footballs is on display at the Surrey Infantry Museum, based at Clandon Park.

The Battle of the Somme also claimed the lives of two Guildford brothers – Tom and Percy Parsons – in the space of seven days. They lived at 5 The Valley, St Catherine's Village. Private Thomas Parsons, The Queen's (Royal West Surrey) Regiment, had enlisted at Stoughton Barracks soon after the outbreak of war. He served with the 5th (Service) Battalion, taking part in the Battle of Loos in June 1915, remaining in the front line until November.

Sergeant Percy Parsons, Royal Field Artillery, enlisted soon after his younger brother, deciding to be a gunner rather than an infantryman. He also fought in the Battle of Loos. He took part in the week-long shelling of the German lines ahead of the start of the Battle of the Somme – a bombardment that ultimately failed to smash the enemy's defences and barbed wire. With Tom billeted in a village alongside the main road to Amines waiting for orders, and Percy with his gun battery, the brothers were only a mile or so apart, although neither would have known.

On 2 July, Tom's battalion was ordered to continue the attacks across 'Mash' valley (so named with army humour to accompany 'Sausage' valley to the south) and take the village of Ovillers. The plan was for a night attack in the early hours of 3 July. Percy's unit was ordered to help in the preparatory barrage for his brother's division. This commenced at 2.15 a.m. Percy would not have known that the shells he was firing would be assisting his younger brother's assault.

Brothers Sergeant Percy Parsons and Private Tom Parsons were killed within seven days of each other during the Battle of the Somme.

Tom probably found that the darkness made the battle even more frightening, making it impossible to see where the next danger might be coming from, while his officers and NCOs would be struggling to command and navigate across the 500 yards of no-man's-land between them and the German trenches. As if all that were not enough, it was raining and there was a thunderstorm to the south east. It was expected that simultaneous attacks of the flanks of Tom's battalion, left and right, would suppress German redoubts that contained many machine-gun posts.

In the event, the attack on the left was postponed at the last moment, allowing German machine-gunners to fire on Tom and his comrades unhindered. Only eight men of The Queen's reached the German wire. By 9 a.m. it was all over; the attack had failed. The 12th Division had suffered 2,400 casualties. The 6th Queen's, the battalion of volunteers that had enlisted at Guildford, had suffered over 300 casualties. Many of those were 'missing, believed killed' and would never have a known grave. One of those was Tom Parsons. Meanwhile, Percy continued to fight just a mile away. He was killed on 10 July and is buried at Bapaume Post Military Cemetery, Albert, France.

One man from Guildford had luck on his side more than once during the war. The parents of Lieutenant G. Garrood, from College Road, were officially notified of his death in the Gallipoli campaign. Badly wounded on the battlefield, he could see but not move or speak. Assumed to be dead, he was about to be buried when it was discovered there was life in him and he was transferred to hospital and recovered. By 1917 he was on active service in German East Africa. He later wrote home to his sister about his remarkable survival in the bush for several days after an aircraft he was flying on a bombing mission crashed. He had many encounters with wild animals, including a leopard, crocodiles, a hippo and some baboons. His letter included: 'My progress was heart-breaking – about 100 yards an hour. My legs were now bare to every thorn, bush and sword grass I passed through, to say nothing of myriads of flies. That day I swam seven streams.'

Bedding down one night, he said he heard a lion about 500 yards away, and he continued: 'At daybreak not fifty yards from the tree under which I slept, I had the annoying experience of surveying two large baboons, the size of small men, quarrelling over my trousers.' He eventually encountered 'two small natives' who 'conducted me to their village'. He went on: 'Arrived at the village I was given a most hospitable reception, and the next day a search party arrived in response to a message from a runner.' Garrood was taken to a field hospital suffering from malaria.

On the night of 26 February 1918, His Majesty's Hospital Ship *Glenard Castle* was torpedoed and sunk within five minutes by a German U-boat off Lundy Island in the Bristol Channel, with the loss of 162 lives and only a few survivors. Two of those killed were from Guildford. The first was Captain L. Moysey of the Royal Army Medical Corps, whose mother lived in Pit Farm Road. He had only joined the ship two days previously. Born in 1869, he had been educated at Repton and Caius College, Cambridge and his name is commemorated on the Hollbrook Memorial in Southampton. The other was Private P. Rodgers, Royal Army Medical Corps, of 2 Falcon Road, aged 26 and a milkman with the Guildford Co-operative Society. His brother, Private J. Rodgers, The Queen's (Royal West Surrey) Regiment, had been reported missing in 1917. His body was never found.

Many men died not in the heat of battle or at sea but in accidents, some in the UK. The *Surrey Times* of 18 May 1918 reported:

> As the result of an accident at the Royal Aircraft Factory, Farnborough on 2 May, Second Air-Mechanic Harold Ernest Lee, son of Pte, and Mrs A.J. Lee, 107 Walnut Tree Close, lost his life. He was at work in the propeller-testing department, and whilst in a stooping position was struck on the head by a propeller, which was doing from 600 to 700 revolutions per minute. The front of his skull was smashed in, and he died soon after admission to the Royal Cambridge Hospital.

Lee was aged 18.

BIG GAME HUNTER SHOT BY A SNIPER

Famous big-game hunter and wild man Frederick Selous of Fox Corner, Worplesdon, was 64 when he was accepted into the Royal Fusiliers. He fought in German East Africa. It's reported that the ace marksman was killed by a sniper's bullet on 4 January 1917.

Pioneer James Knight, 47, was killed near Ypres, Belgium, June 1917. His son, Lance Corporal Robert Charles Knight, died one year later while fighting in France.

A Burpham woman was not only widowed when her husband was killed but, a year later, lost a son too. Clara Knight received the news that her husband James, aged 47, died on active service on 5 June 1917. The family, that included five children, had moved to Bowers Cottages, Burpham, by the time of the 1911 census. On it, James' occupation is listed as 'groundsman, golf links'. However, he had also been a policeman at Godstone in Surrey.

Enlisting at Westminster, he served with the Royal Engineers in the 6th Army Tramway Company. He most likely worked on the narrow-gauge railways that transported ammunition and supplies to front-line troops and the wounded back from the dressing stations. He is buried at Bard Cottage Cemetery near Ypres in Belgium.

Lance Corporal Robert Charles Knight was the eldest son. He enlisted at Winchester and first served in France with the Rifle Brigade before transferring to the Machine Gun Corps, ultimately losing his life on 17 June 1918. Official records state that he died as opposed to being 'killed in action' or having 'died of wounds'. Therefore, he may have succumbed to sickness or disease. He is buried in Premont British Cemetery, Aisne, France.

His widowed mother Clara later moved to Merrow and died in 1925 after being hit by a motorcyclist in Trodds Lane. James and Robert are commemorated on the war memorial in St Luke's church, Burpham, with Clara's grave close by.

On the Western Front during the spring of 1918, the Germans made one final massive offensive, gaining a good deal of ground from the Allies and taking many prisoners, with thousands of casualties on both sides. But the German army could not sustain its own heavy losses and the tide began to turn in favour of the Allies. Through the summer and into the autumn, British, French and American troops pushed the Germans back until the end was in sight. But many men were to lose their lives right up until the end.

Lance Corporal Charles Tubbs of The Queen's (Royal West Surrey) Regiment was gassed in France. He died in a field hospital near Dieppe a month before the Armistice in 1918.

One of the last of Guildford's heroes to die shortly before the Armistice on 11 November 1918 (and there were more who had been injured who died afterwards) was Lance Corporal Charles Tubbs of The Queen's (Royal West Surrey) Regiment, and the great uncle of the author of this book. The *Surrey Advertiser* reported that he died on 2 October 1918 from mustard gas poisoning and that he was educated at Stoke School, adding that before he joined up in October 1915, Tubbs was employed as a grocer. His sister, Eva Rose (née Tubbs), the author's grandmother, was informed of his death at her home at 7 Falcon Road. It is likely that he died at a field hospital near Dieppe, and is buried at the nearby Mount Huon Military Cemetery at Le Treport. He was aged just 21.

A TANK NAMED *GUILDFORD*
Second Lieutenant H. Puttock of Guildford, wrote home:
'I went into action commanding H.M.L.S. "Guildford".
This name was selected by the crew, who were nearly all trained at Bisley. A shell hit us and set us on fire, but we managed to get out.'

Shot for Desertion: Second Lieutenant Eric Skeffington Poole

During the First World War, the British executed 306 men for desertion and cowardice. Only two of those were officers, one being Second Lieutenant Eric Skeffington Poole, whose name is on the Guildford war memorial.

Born in Nova Scotia in 1885, Poole served with the 63rd Regiment of the Halifax Rifles, between 1903 and 1905. The Poole family arrived in Guildford sometime between 1905 and 1914. The address of 2 Rectory Place, off Portsmouth Road, appears on details about Poole, recorded by the Commonwealth War Graves Commission. Military documents from October 1914 give his address as 'Spreyton' (Joseph's Road), Guildford.

He joined the Honourable Artillery Company as a driver in B Reserve Battery, and was commissioned on 3 May 1915. At the end of May 1916, Poole joined the 11th Battalion West Yorkshire Regiment and went to France.

The medical history sheet compiled for Poole's court martial reveals that he suffered 'shell shock' after being hit by clods of earth distributed by an enemy shell on the Somme on 7 July 1916, but returned to duty at the end of August. In his testimony for his trial, Poole wrote that he often became confused and had great difficulty making up his mind. He wandered away from the frontline on 5 October 1916 and, two days later, was apprehended by the military police.

Charged with desertion, Poole's trial took place at Poperinghe, Belgium, on 24 November 1916. Of six witnesses, two spoke for his defence. A Royal Army Medical Corps officer said that Poole's mental condition had precluded him from intentionally deserting his company.

Despite this, he was found guilty and executed by firing squad at Poperinghe Town Hall on 10 December 1916. He lies in the town's military cemetery. General Haig is reported as saying that, although Poole was an officer, no exceptions could be made owing to his rank.

Second Lieutenant Eric Skeffington Poole was shot for desertion on 10 December 1916.

5

WHILE YOU'RE AWAY

Throughout the First World War, Britain's farmers were constantly being urged to cultivate more land to grow more produce. However, by 1916 local farmers and growers found themselves in some difficulty. Many had lost valuable men to the services, meaning there was a shortage of people to operate farm equipment such as threshing machines, while the machines themselves were not being serviced and were therefore prone to breaking down. Furthermore, the cost of animal feed and seeds was ever increasing.

By 1917, women were being employed on the land, even by the most reluctant of farmers.

In January 1917, questions were asked as to whether German prisoners of war who were imprisoned near Frimley in Surrey could be made to work on local farms. Inquiries were made and seventy-five were soon at work, scattered across West Surrey farms. Twelve of these worked at Guildford's sewage works at Slyfield, where land was used for growing crops.

Opinion was divided among farmers as to the use of female labour, but increasingly they were being employed even by the most reluctant of farmers – albeit for tending horses and cattle rather than working machinery or doing more strenuous work. In March 1917, Surrey's local newspapers published a letter that called for more farmers to assist in training women for work on the land. They were also urged to provide board and lodging for the women while they trained. Any farmer who was willing to take part, and householders who could also offer accommodation, were asked to supply details to the Surrey Women's War Agricultural Committee, which had offices in North Street, Guildford. By the summer of 1917 there were 1,000 women working full time and 994 part time on Surrey farms.

A New Zealander by birth, Noeline Baker took charge of the Surrey Division of the Women's Land Army. Before the war, she had been active in the National Union of Women's Suffrage Societies and a founder member of her local branch. In 1920 she was made an MBE for her wartime work.

The Surrey Division of the Women's Land Army held a rally in Guildford in October 1917. Its aim was to encourage others to join the workforce, and 110 women took part, parading through the town behind a group of pipers from a Canadian regiment. The *Surrey Times* reported:

Dressed in long drill coats and corduroy breeches, with gaiters or leggings and strong serviceable boots, and wearing picturesque wide-brimmed felt hats, they looked quite capable of doing a hard day's work on the farm. The glow of health radiated from their faces, and evidently to them life is full of happiness.

LANDWORKERS' AFTERNOON IN TOWN.

25 October 1917

A few of the 200 happy girl land-workers who have been addressed at Borough Hall, Guildford, by the Hon. Mrs. Lyttelton, of the Women's Land Army—(*Daily Sketch* Photograph)

The Surrey division of the Women's Land Army held a rally in Guildford in October 1917.

The event included a meeting at the County and Borough Hall. There, the assistant director of the Women's Branch of the Board of Agriculture, the Hon. Mrs Lyttelton, commented in her speech that when 'the boys' came home from the trenches they would say 'well done' to the land girls. She expressed the hope that their work would see a change in agriculture, and if anyone who had served in the Women's Land Army wanted to remain in farming, the government 'would advance money and plant to settle them'.

But as 1917 drew to a close, it was becoming more obvious that Britain was facing a dire food crisis. This had come about despite calls in April of that year for Britain to adopt a voluntary system of food rationing. This was followed in May by a royal proclamation, calling for people not to use flour in any product other than bread. The result in Guildford was that during the following week, demand for bread fell. At the workhouse in Warren Road, the Board of Guardians instructed that rice and oatmeal should be used more often, so as to save flour and bread.

Following a national directive, Guildford council set up its Food Control Committee in August 1917. It immediately brought complaints from shopkeepers, none of whom were represented. To address matters, a Consultative Trade Committee was formed that included representatives from local dairymen, butchers and grocers, to work in conjunction with the Food Control Committee. As a result, butchers were instructed to clearly displays prices in their shops, while maximum prices were fixed for meat, butter, flour, bread and jam. Special applications had to be made for extra supplies of sugar, and could only be used by people producing jam and preserves from fruit growing in their gardens or allotments, or gathered from the countryside. Approximately 1,000 applications were soon received from the people of Guildford.

The north side of Guildford High Street, with the Maypole Dairy store and butchers Colebrook & Co. Both were in the news at the end of 1917 as the crisis over food shortages worsened.

However, despite these measures, the food crisis deepened and by November 1917 ever-growing queues of people could be seen waiting outside Guildford's food shops such as Sainsbury's, Lipton's, the Maypole Dairy, Home & Colonial Stores and Gates' West Surrey Central Dairy Company. Butter, margarine, tea, sugar and preserves were the main goods that were in short supply. This was a completely new spectacle in the town, as people of all classes and backgrounds were forming the queues. The scheme to fix prices failed to ensure an even supply of food and it meant that Christmas 1917 was, for most, a miserable one indeed. The usual displays in shop windows of seasonal goodies and treats were visibly absent to those who stood in the queues. Many had to do without Christmas puddings as the ingredients were simply not available.

Guildford's cattle market in Woodbridge Road witnessed extraordinary scenes in January 1918. A ballot was introduced for the bidding on the few beasts there being offered for sale.

But it was meat that suddenly disappeared from the shops come January 1918. New regulations had been introduced for the sale and price of cattle and their allocation at market. At Guildford cattle market on 1 January 1918, there were just thirty-nine beasts for sale – and a lot of prospective buyers. Under the conditions of the government order, the animals were balloted for (slips of paper were draw from an enamelled jug),

meaning that many buyers ended up with no chance of buying any meat at all that day. And as they were restricted to which markets they could attend to buy from, many ended the week unable to purchase any at all.

News of the crisis at the cattle market soon spread, and many Guildfordians who thronged the town's butchers on the Saturday for their weekend joints came away with nothing. As the 'sold out' signs began appearing, the crowds rushed to the fishmongers and shops selling cold meat in an attempt to buy there. Soon they were also displaying the ubiquitous 'sold out' signs, while the grocery stores were next, selling out of tinned fish that was already in limited supply.

It got worse the following weekend that afterwards was dubbed 'Jointless Sunday'. There were seventy-four beasts offered for sale at the cattle market on the Tuesday before, but more dealers than the previous week were present wanting to buy. It was decided to allocate the animals to areas in and around Guildford based on population. Guildford district secured eleven, while three went to Godalming and four to Woking. A ballot was used to divide up the rest. But there was still not enough meat to go around and some Guildford butchers ended up with not a scrap of meat at all to sell. Supplies were getting so short that butchers announced that they would neither sell nor deliver on Wednesdays until further notice.

Another crisis soon followed, this time involving the supply of butter. Tension had been building between traders and Guildford's Food Control Committee over the way the committee was operating. There were accusations that some traders were infringing the regulations, while the committee was not doing enough to look into the matter, or turning a blind eye. On the other hand, members of the committee had been unfairly harassing some shopkeepers. On the morning of Saturday, 12 January, Gates' store pulled down its shutters in protest, claiming the food committee had unfairly summoned its manager, Mr G. Bowyer, on the count that its shop was refusing to sell butter (made by its own West Surrey Central Dairy Company) to customers unless they bought other goods as well. Gates' denied the claim and took its protest further by announcing that it would stop producing butter forthwith – which, as it noted, it was losing money on anyway, due to the system of price fixing.

There were calls for the mayor (William Shawcross) to resign as chairman of the Food Control Committee, but he refused. The committee then met and passed a vote of confidence in him. This set off a chain of events that included a number of employees of Dennis Bros' motorworks, machine-tool makers Drummonds and local railwaymen marching on the Guildhall on Saturday, 26 January to complain of alleged practices that butchers were holding back meat for more wealthy customers. They were invited in to meet with members of the food committee, where the protesters suggested that butchers should open on alternate days, instead of all closing on Mondays, Tuesdays and Wednesdays; that no meat should be reserved; and all customers should be served on a first come, first served basis.

At the time of the food crisis, there were calls for the chairman of Guildford's Food Control Committee, Mayor William Shawcross, to resign.

The town's butchers agreed to these suggestions and the dispute with Gates' West Surrey Central Dairy Company was dropped, the firm promising to resume butter production. Four days later, a decision was made to dissolve the food committee

and appoint a new one. Although the mayor and a number of other councillors sat on the new committee, it also featured the Labour party candidate for Guildford, William Bennett, and others representing the 'working classes' of the town. At once it set to work and passed a voluntary scheme whereby each person in Guildford was limited to 4oz of butter and margarine a week and 8oz of meat from a butcher. It was introduced as a temporary scheme, as it was known that compulsory rationing was on its way.

That day came on Monday, 25 February, when every household received a ration book for each person living at that address. Meat, butter and margarine were

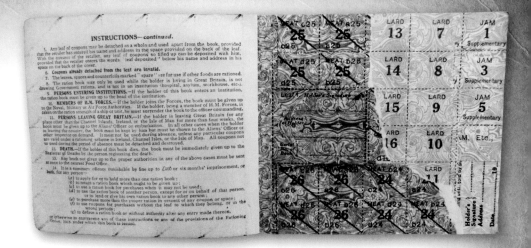

Ration books were issued in Britain on 25 February 1918.

the first items rationed, to be followed later by bacon, jam, tea, sugar and lard. Ration books contained coupons and, as an example, each adult was allowed to use three coupons per week for meat (children under 10 had two coupons) – each valued at 5*s* each. Householders had to choose the shops they would go to for various foods and, once registered, were not permitted to change without permission. If people had to travel away from Guildford, they were allowed to take their ration books with them.

The town's Food Control Office issued 26,000 ration books. It had the enormous task of liaising with retailers, who in turn had to keep detailed records of customers and the supply of commodities. A mountain of paperwork went back and forth, with the office also having to send records to the Food Controller in London.

For those who did the family shopping, food rationing and the books with their coupons took some getting used to. Many misjudgements were made as people surrendered their coupons too soon, only to realise they would have to do without until the following week, and so on. The ration books also had to be used when purchasing from restaurants. Some of these in Guildford soon found that customers were refraining from buying meals with meat in, preferring to keep their coupons for their next visit to the butcher.

WAITER! WHERE IS MY PORTION OF SUGAR? IT WAS THERE JUST NOW SIR. I EXPECT THAT FLY MUST HAVE EATEN IT.

A picture postcard poking fun at the wartime shortage of sugar.

Food was still scarce, despite the introduction of compulsory rationing – especially potatoes – during the first half of 1918. But it did result in a fairer distribution of food and the queues outside shops ceased soon after rationing was introduced.

Guildford's most infamous night during the war was on Wednesday, 13 October 1915, when a Zeppelin airship of Germany's Imperial Navy circled over Guildford, dropping twelve bombs on St Catherine's Village and Shalford Park. This was Guildford's night of terror, and one that those who witnessed the events would not have forgotten for the rest of their lives. That afternoon, five airships left their German bases at Nordholtz and Hage. Their aim was to fly over the Norfolk coast and attack London from the north. One airship got lost over Norfolk and headed for home, but the others continued and dropped bombs in the London area. In most cases, though, they failed to hit their intended targets. The blackout in force across Britain made navigation extremely difficult.

The commander of the Zeppelin L13, Heinrich Mathy, was in charge of the whole raid. This experienced and heroic commander and his crew dropped bombs over the site of an anti-aircraft gun near Hatfield in Hertfordshire and then picked up the Thames on their way to bomb the waterworks at Hampton.

It appears that while over Weybridge, Mathy missed a vital bend in the Thames and headed down the River Wey instead, passing places such as Newark and Send.

THE FATE OF ZEPPELIN COMMANDER HEINRICH MATHY

Kapitänleutnant Mathy, who commanded the German Zeppelin that bombed St Catherine's, died on 1 October 1916 when his airship was shot down over Hertfordshire. On 10 September 1916, the people of Guildford could see flames from another airship also shot down over that county in the night sky.

The L13 reached Guildford at about 10 p.m., where it circled for a time then flew off in the direction of Wood Street, before returning to Guildford and St Catherine's Village. Once there, a brilliant blue flare was dropped from the airship.

At 10.25 p.m., another flare was dropped that also lit up the sky. Then its bombs were released. The L13 made off in an easterly direction towards Redhill, turned towards London again and dropped further bombs on Woolwich Arsenal, mistaking it for the Victoria Docks. Mathy and his crew finally got back to their base the next morning.

The German Imperial Navy Zeppelin airship L13 that visited Guildford on 13 October 1915.

The other Zeppelins in the raid dropped their bombs in a variety of locations and caused a good deal of damage. In all they dropped 102 explosive bombs and eighty-seven incendiary bombs, killing seventy-one people and injuring 128. In Croydon alone, fifty-three people died.

It would have been the sound of the airship's droning engines that people in Guildford first heard when the L13 was overhead on that infamous night. Some people may have seen the flares dropped by the Zeppelin's crew – but just about everybody would have heard the bombs exploding. Those who ventured outdoors would certainly have caught a glimpse of the airship. And the following day, many people went to St Catherine's to see what had happened.

The Zeppelin dropped twelve bombs across St Catherine's Village. A wall of the outside toilet at the Hope and Anchor pub in Portsmouth Road was blown down, leaving the landlord's wife terrified and exposed!

Evidence of blast damage. Part of a wall beside the towpath of the River Wey near St Catherine's has never been rebuilt.

Mercifully, no one died but there was a lot of damage to buildings – such as smashed windows and walls that had collapsed – and the main railway line was damaged between the two tunnels. But many people would have suffered from shock, especially those living in St Catherine's.

The Guildford police constabulary report noted where each bomb fell and the damage done:

Bomb 1:   fell in the garden of Little Croft, Guildown Road. It uprooted a large tree and made a crater 3ft deep and 20ft wide. A garden gate was blown away and 146 panes of glass were broken.

Bomb 2:   fell in a field belonging to Braboeuf Farm. It made a hole 3ft deep and 10ft wide.

Bomb 3:   fell in Chestnut Avenue at the rear of Guildown Grange. It made a hole in the roadway 3ft deep and 8ft wide. A wall 8ft high and 21ft long was knocked down. Much damage was done to a greenhouse.

Bomb 4: also fell in Chestnut Avenue, making a hole 3ft deep and 10ft in diameter. Approximately 30 yards of garden fencing was blown away.

Bomb 5: fell in garden of St Catherine's Cottage, making a hole 3ft deep and 20ft in diameter. Twenty-two panes of glass were broken in a greenhouse and the roof of the main house was badly damaged. At nearby Montague House, seventy-four panes of glass were broken. Blast from this bomb also caused damage to Langton Priory (sixty-two panes of glass), and the Hope and Anchor pub, where 105 panes of glass were smashed.

Bomb 6: fell at the up side of the railway line about 120 yards from the chalk tunnel. It made a large hole in the ground and cut pieces out of the rails. A signal post was also damaged.

Bomb 7: fell in a chicken run belonging to a Mr Hudson of The Beacon. Seventeen fowls were killed.

Bomb 8: fell at the bottom of the chicken run, making a hole about 4ft deep and 10ft in diameter. Approximately 20ft of brick and stone walling were blown away. [The gap in the wall beside the towpath of the River Wey can be seen to this day.]

Bomb 9: fell on the east side of the River Wey, breaking telephone wires and damaging the riverbank.

Bomb 10: fell about 60 yards on the same side of the river towards Guildford. It brought down a telephone post and wire and killed a swan.

Bombs 11 and 12: fell in Shalford Park – then a nine-hole golf course. One fell on the seventh green and the other about 50 yards away, both making large holes. It's believed a fragment of the last bomb struck the shutter of Tollgate Cottage on the Shalford Road.

A letter written by a resident of York Road to a soldier serving overseas was penned an hour after L13 left the Guildford area:

I heard plainly enough the tremendous strumming of an airship, sounding like a bluebottle's buzz magnified a thousand or two times. I thought at first it was one of our own airships from Farnborough out experimenting on a night trip. It was a beautiful starlit night, but I could not for a time see any airship. Now and again there was a brilliant flare, and then you could see the long rays of a searchlight. Even then I could not believe it was a Zepp. For some minutes I watched while the thing seemed to go to and fro. Suddenly there was a flash and a terrific bang, followed at quick intervals by others, which literally made the ground shake. We had a Zeppelin with us at last! I at once left the insecure shelter of the lawn in case of falling bullets; and as I was going in a special constable came rushing down the road yelling, 'All lights out.' I went out again on to the lawn, and again the bombs boomed, causing the windows to rattle and the house seemed to shake to its foundations. Then I saw it. It was the usual thing so often described – cigar-shaped, and at such a height that it looked just like a cigar against the luminous star-lit sky. At this time, looking almost straight up above the lawn, its position seemed to be such that if it had dropped a bomb it would have fallen 200 or 300 yards away in the direction of Pewley Hill. I went out – there were heaps of people about in the road – and down to the police station. The town was in absolute darkness. Special constables were hurrying up from all directions, and parading outside the police station. The fire brigade was out ready for emergencies. I remained about a quarter of an hour, but by that time no word had come of any fires in Guildford or district. So I went home again to find people standing about everywhere, some in their night things. What a topic of conversation for tomorrow!

GIRLS AND MEN IN KHAKI

Concerns were raised in the local press in the spring of 1916 about large numbers of local girls seen fraternising with soldiers in punts and rowing boats on the river. Calling it a scandal, the report noted that many were not returning until midnight.

Telephone inquiries were soon coming through to Guildford from Oxford, Reading and other places asking the whereabouts of the Zeppelin.

At the Royal Surrey County Hospital in Farnham Road, all the lights were switched off and there was alarm among the civilian patients, while it was later reported that the soldier patients took the visit of the Zeppelin more philosophically, and even joked about it. A Charles Hodgson, who lived at Shamley Green, told William Oakley (the then editor of the *Surrey Advertiser*) that no bombs would have been dropped on Guildford had the Zeppelin not been alerted by the 'popguns' firing at it from the Chilworth gunpowder works.

A Mr Jacobs of Guildford, meanwhile, took a measurement of the Zeppelin and estimated that when it was over the town it was at about 9,600ft. A William Harvey told the *Surrey Advertiser* that the Zeppelin was quite low when it first appeared over the town, but rose rapidly to a great height after it had dropped the first flare. In the brilliant light of the flare he said he could see the windows of the airship and what he believed to be faces looking out.

Such were the reporting restrictions in place at the time that none of Guildford's local newspapers were able to report the event – yet it was the biggest story they had probably seen in living memory. In 1983, the then curator of Guildford Museum, Matthew Alexander, interviewed Ernest Yates, who was born in Guildford in 1906, and who recalled the Zeppelin raid:

It was a clear moonlit night and I awoke suddenly to the sound of loud, excited voices, some raised in anger, in the road outside our house … Many families were there clothed in a sketchy fashion, all of them gazing upwards. The cause of all this uproar was the unmistakable shape of a Zeppelin silhouetted in the moonlight like a cigar suspended in space. Its movement appeared slow at such an altitude. Everyone was wondering what might happen, when argument was translated into action. Our next-door neighbour shinned up a lamp-post with the intention of putting out the gaslight. After much puffing and blowing, this burly middle-aged man achieved his object, to the applause of those below.

FLAG DAYS
Street collections
in Guildford raised
generous sums for
wartime causes.
For example, 'Sick and
Wounded Horses Day'
raised £396, 'Sailors'
Day' £500, 'Prisoners
of War Day' £425,
and 'Red Cross Day' £382.

St Catherine's resident Tom Parsons remembers shrapnel from the raid being embedded in the boiler house and potting shed building in the south-east corner of St Catherine's Nursery (where Turnham Close now exists). The shrapnel was still there until the buildings were taken down in the 1980s, when Coombs Garage purchased the site.

A story has passed down the descendants of a Mr Rowlands, who was the landlord of the Hope and Anchor pub. When the raid took place, his wife was sitting on the outside toilet. She sat tight as the bombs began to explode until the blast of the fifth bomb, exploding just across the Portsmouth Road, took down the walls of the outhouse, leaving the poor woman exposed and terrified!

A blast from what is believed to have been the sixth bomb caused damage to some of the cottages in The Valley, breaking tiles and windows. A long-term effect was caused by the collapse of some of the lime plaster ceilings inside several of those cottages. During the repair work, the collapsed plaster was spread on the shared walkways around the cottages. A former resident, Elsie Oldroyd, used to complain that even after the Second World War, her children would walk it into the house when it had been wet outside.

A postcard sent from Woking to Rochester in Kent and postmarked 15 October, two days after the raid on Guildford, notes that the bombs that fell at St Catherine's seem to have been heard as far away as Woking. It reads: 'Were you very upset Wed night. Did you see or hear Zepps. They were all around us. Heard bombs dropping.'

A postcard sent to an address in Kent two days after the raid on Guildford stated the explosions were heard as far away as Woking. The recipient was asked whether they were afraid and if they had heard anything.

The Chilworth Gunpowder Mills were guarded by a detachment of the 2/5th Battalion of The Queen's (Royal West Surrey) Regiment. Captain James Ness of No. 3 Supernumerary Company of The Queen's wrote to the commander in chief, Eastern Command, at Horse Guards in London.

> I report that at 10.05 p.m. last night an airship was heard approaching, and was shortly discerned at a great height approaching from the east and moving directly over the factory. It moved and made a circle over the factory then continued its journey west. The airship returned to the western boundary then turned again west, and shortly afterwards we heard some ten or twelve explosions in the direction of Guildford. The airship again returned to the factory, flew over the western position and disappeared in a south easterly direction. As soon as the airship was seen, I ordered all lights out at the factory and work ceased. I at once telephoned the Royal Flying Corps at Farnborough. Later on I tried to telephone elsewhere, but found I could not get through, the wires being down between Chilworth and Guildford [having been destroyed by the explosions]. I sent a messenger by bicycle into Guildford and am pleased to be able to report that nobody had been hurt, although a certain amount of material damage was done. Some of the soldiers guarding the gunpowder works fired their rifles at the airship as did the anti-aircraft detachment that was also stationed there.

In its official report, it seems as if its commander was trying to make out his gunners were unlucky not to have brought the airship down. Captain James Ness continued: 'Rapid fire was continued until she was obscured. It is thought that she was hit at least once, as a shower of fire was seen near her. We fired seventy-seven rounds and were much handicapped by having no night tracers nor searchlights.'

PUB OPENING HOURS REDUCED
Soon after the outbreak of war, pubs in Guildford were ordered to close at 9 p.m. instead of 11 p.m., and it was forbidden to sell bottled beer to soldiers. Later, all British pubs were forced to close during the afternoon, a law that was not repealed until 1988.

Borough of Guildford.

RULES FOR THE

Safety of the General Public

IN CASE OF

AIR RAIDS.

To those who happen to be in the Street.

Take cover immediately. There is danger from bombs from aircraft, also from fragments of shells and bullets, etc., from guns used against aircraft. The assembly of crowds is very dangerous, and might prove fatal. The nearest basement would be the safest place. Any fragments of shells should be handed to the Police, for the purpose of being forwarded to the War Office for expert examination. Unexploded bombs must not be touched, but information respecting them should be given to the Police at once. Do not strike matches to light pipes, etc., nor use electric hand-lamps. Obey orders given by the Police quickly.

To those in Private Houses.

Stay there—preferably on the ground floor, but, should there be a cellar, in the cellar. Provide yourselves with matches, candles, or electric hand-lamps, and turn out lights. Be prepared for electricity being turned off at works. Should gas be turned off at the works, or should you turn off gas at meter, see all gas burner taps are properly turned off before the gas is turned on again. Stand away from walls lest they fall on you.

One thing NOT to do.

Do not rush out of the house to see what is going on.

SPECIAL WARNING TO ALL.

Read new Lighting Order of the 21st October, 1915, posted throughout the Borough, and act accordingly. **This Order will be strictly enforced.**

Expert opinion is against warning by blowing of syrens or ringing of bells in case of air raid. It has been decided to discontinue such warnings in Guildford in future.

G. S. ODLING-SMEE,

25th October, 1915. **Mayor.**

MILLS & SONS, Printers, Castle Street, Guildford.

Twelve days after the Zeppelin's visit, Guildford council published a poster advising the public on what they should do in the event of an air raid.

A letter written by the occupant of Guildown House two days after the raid notes that he had just put his mother to bed when the first bomb fell in a garden at the end of his lawn, blowing his windows in.

Evidently, his mother was 'splendid' as the bombs fell and the house rocked. He then filled the bath with water and watched what he thought were two Zeppelins passing over his house. There was only ever one. He continued his letter, explaining where the bombs fell and that his mother then had a 'heart attack' – so he gave her a tablet and 'watched the Zepps on their way home'.

But why bomb Guildford? It has been suggested that the L13's commander, Heinrich Mathy, knew about Chilworth Gunpowder Mills and was trying to bomb them. As previously stated, when the gunners at Chilworth saw the airship that night they opened fire. This would have alerted Mathy and his crew, indicating to them that they were over a target of some importance, and is surely why flares and the twelve bombs were dropped. However, in his log written shortly after the raid, Mathy reported that he had bombed the waterworks at Hampton on the Thames. It is therefore almost certain that he was just completely lost.

THE VOLUNTEER TRAINING CORPS

Men who were too old for active service but wanted to do something for the war effort joined the Volunteer Training Corps. Guildford's corps attracted men from all backgrounds, plus a few younger men engaged in war work but who also wanted to offer their services.

The first commandant of the corps was a Colonel A.V. Hatch. Under his leadership, the men met two or three evenings a week and sometimes at weekends at the Drill Hall in Sandfield Terrace, where they had instruction in rifle shooting on its miniature range. In its early days the men had no uniforms or equipment. It was discovered that, somehow, Guildford council had in its possession some rifles from the Boer War, and these were generously loaned along with a gift of £50 for expenses.

Uniforms of a grey-green material arrived in 1915, with most men paying for their own. Later red armbands with the letters 'G.R.' (Georgius Rex) were issued. This led to some public ridicule and jokes that the letters stood for 'Grandpa's Regiment' or 'Government Rejects'.

The Guildford Training Corps went through a number of changes during the war, first becoming the 6th Battalion Surrey Volunteer Regiment and by the time of disbanding in 1919, the 3rd Battalion The Queen's (Royal West Surrey) Regiment.

The naturalist and writer Eric Parker (1870–1955) was the commanding officer with the Volunteer Training Corps, patrolling the Chilworth Gunpowder Mills, which he described as 'the most monotonous work that has ever come my way'. The patrol took him past eleven sentries, with their boxes placed around the circumference of the factory. He later wrote: 'Going the rounds on a moonlight night was an easy enough task, but on a cloudy or rainy night, you had to know your paths through fields and woods pretty accurately.'

*Men of the Guildford Training Corps pictured at Allen House
(now the site of the Royal Grammar School) in October 1915.*

6

COMING HOME

Throughout the war Guildford gave so much; in terms of the men who made the supreme sacrifice, its help to the sick and wounded and those who worked tirelessly producing munitions and working on the land, while Guildfordians dug deep in their pockets, helping to finance the conflict through street collections and buying war bonds. This continued until a month before the Armistice.

The government encouraged people to buy bonds and savings certificates, and towns and cities throughout Britain held events – sometimes lasting a week or more – that urged people and businesses to contribute in whatever way they could.

A vacant plot of land off Guildford High Street was transformed into a very realistic Western Front trench system. Called 'Flanders in Moonlight', it was part of the town's Feed The Guns Week.

The War Savings Certificate scheme took place in 1916, followed by The Victory Loan in 1917. Banners were hung across the High Street and posters were displayed in shop windows with slogans such as 'They have given their lives, won't you lend your money?' The money did indeed pour in, with a staggering £2 million subscribed from within the wider Guildford area. Some people used hitherto forgotten gold sovereigns they had stashed away at home. Between them, three banks in Guildford exchanged more than £1,200 worth of gold for bonds, with its post offices tendering sovereigns to the value of £4,312.

The town's businessmen also contributed by buying National War Bonds or War Savings Certificates, while urging residents to do the same. Guildford held Businessmen's Week, also called War Plane Week, in March 1918, with the aim of raising £62,500 – enough to 'buy' twenty-five aeroplanes. Once again, the town was full of posters and promotional material in shop windows; one display featured a model plane that was illuminated at night. Large banners proclaimed, 'War planes help our cause to thrive; Guildford must have twenty-five' and 'Guildford buys the war planes gladly; Willie gets the wind up badly'. A number of Royal Flying Corps aircraft flew over the town daily during the campaign, performing acrobatics and dropping leaflets that urged people to subscribe.

A street collection in Guildford for Our Day, held in October 1918, raised £1,391. The total included one donation of £500.

The local press reported:

> …just after one o'clock the hum of engines in the air was heard, and a few seconds later a two-seater and a single-seater came into view. After encircling around the town the pilots proceeded to give a thrilling exhibition of their skill. The spectators stood with baited breath as they watched nosedives from the clouds, with engine shut off a rapid succession of loops and porpoise movements. The machines travelled at a terrific pace, and at times were so low as just to skim over the roofs of the houses.

It all had the desired effect: the target was hit and surpassed in just two days, with £69,000 pledged. Guildford received a letter from George V, thanking everyone for their support, which was soon printed up and copies distributed. It too helped the cause, as the final total was a staggering £273,000. The greater part of the money came via local businesses such as Dennis Bros (which subscribed £20,000), the Friary Brewery (£10,000), and the Castle Brewery (£8,000).

The war was slowly coming to an end. Throughout the summer and into the autumn of 1918, the Allies were pushing the Germans back on the Western Front. Meanwhile in Britain, the war loan campaigns continued. During Feed the Guns Week from 21–26 October, just short of the Armistice, Guildford did something rather spectacular, creating a very realistic mock-up portion of a Western Front trench system, complete with sandbags, dugouts, a dressing station and even a bomb-damaged church's crypt with an improvised high altar.

It was Councillor H. Fentum-Phillips, President of the Guildford Chamber of Trade, who came up with the idea, which followed on from his leading efforts during War Plane Week. The trench system display was named 'Flanders in Moonlight', and the committee he formed included as its treasurer the appropriately named Mr W.P. Trench!

It was sited on a vacant plot of land off the High Street, where Tunsgate Square Shopping Centre is today. The plot had been the site of draper Reeks & Co., whose premises had been destroyed by fire in 1915. Canadian soldiers stationed at nearby Witley Camp erected the trench system that included 20,000 sandbags. When opened, people flocked to it, to walk along the duckboards, past signs that stated things such as 'Keep Low – Sniper', and 'Mined', only to come fact to face with a camouflaged six-inch howitzer. Here, those who bought bonds and certificates had their paper-work officially stamped.

AN OPEN SPACE FOR ALL
In 'thankfulness for the conclusion of the Great War', Guildford's Friary Brewery bought the 21-acre Pewley Down close to the town centre and gifted it as an open space for all to enjoy. A plinth at the beauty spot commemorates this.

Local VADs manned the 'dressing station' and there was signalling equipment set up and linked to the keep in the Castle Grounds. By the end of the first day, £90,000 had been subscribed and by the end of the week £287,197 had poured in, easily surpassing the original target by some £30,000. Again, big businesses and banks made up the bulk of the certificates bought, with the National Deposit Friendly Society subscribing £30,000, Lloyds and Capital and Counties Bank £25,000, Dennis Bros £20,000, and the Boys of the Royal Grammar School (or more likely their parents) chipping in with a total of £1,360.

As early as September 1918, Germany had approached the Allies about an Armistice. Crippled by the human cost of losing so many men on the battlefield, Germany faced political and economic strife at home and rumours of a revolution. The terms of the Armistice were communicated on Friday, 8 November, which Germany had seventy-two hours to accept or reject. The following day, Guildford received official news that the Kaiser had resigned. The Armistice was signed at 5.10 a.m. on 11 November, becoming effective at 11 a.m. Only then did the guns fall silent. Later that morning, people rushed into Guildford to read the news displayed outside local newspaper offices.

People flocked to walk along the duckboards of the trench system that contained 20,000 sandbags. Beside a camouflaged six-inch howitzer, those who bought bonds and certificates had their paperwork stamped.

As the bells of Holy Trinity and St Nicolas' churches rang out, flags and ribbons were hung from buildings and people cheered King George V and the gallant servicemen of the Allied forces.

Soon, large crowds were gathering that included wounded soldiers from the local war hospitals. Dressed in their blue uniforms, they formed a procession and made their way through the town centre, singing popular wartime songs.

Next it was the turn of the new Mayor of Guildford, Mr W.S. Tavener, to read the official declaration of the Armistice from the balcony of the Guildhall, at noon. As the crowds gathered in the High Street waiting to hear the mayor, the singing continued with a Canadian officer, using his cane as a baton, conducting the tunes. Then there was much cheering as the mayor, councillors and other dignitaries walked on to the balcony. A few notes played on a bugle by a scoutmaster was followed by the Suffragan Bishop of Guildford, the Rt Revd John Randolf, offering praise and prayers – at which everyone in the crowd removed their hats. He prayed that 'we might become more worthy as a nation, that we might ever remember those who had laid down their lives or who had been maimed'.

The Mayor of Guildford at the time of the Armistice was W.S. Taverner, who owned a pharmacy in the High Street.

The proclamation was duly read out, followed by more cheers. The mayor said all everyone wanted to say: 'thank God that peace has come.'

By this time even more people were flocking to the town centre as factories, other businesses and schools closed for the day that had been announced a public holiday. That evening, members of the council attended a special service of thanksgiving at Holy Trinity church. Before the rain that began to fall in the afternoon started to disperse the crowds somewhat, there was one more spectacle: a line of soldiers marched down the High Street with an effigy of

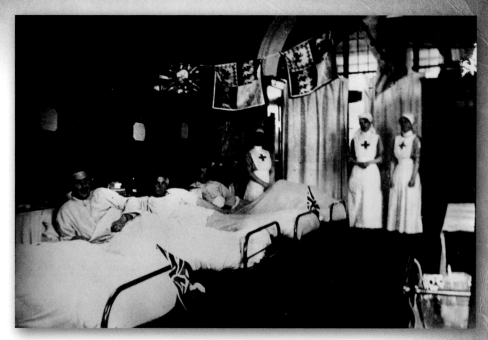

the Kaiser soaked in a flammable spirit. They stopped opposite the Guildhall and the effigy was ceremoniously set alight with more cheers ringing out.

Soon, people's thoughts turned to when servicemen would be returning home. As men from Guildford had been serving in many different locations around the world, their return would be sporadic. However, the town was determined to offer a heroes' welcome as and when they returned home. The first to arrive back were officers and men from The Queen's (Royal West Surrey) Regiment, who had been prisoners of war. A total of 280, who either lived in Guildford or had enlisted locally, were invited to a 'welcome home' event on 25 January 1919. They assembled at the railway station and marched to the Guildhall behind their regiment's band playing the tune 'See, The Conquering Hero Comes'. Again, well-wishers lined the streets. The mayor and members of the council met the soldiers at the Guildhall, and from there they marched to the Borough Hall in North Street, where they were greeted by the Lord Lieutenant and the High Sheriff of Surrey, as well as other dignitaries. They all sat down together for tea and the soldiers were presented with a bronze medal.

This photograph was taken on Armstice Day itself, and flags have been hung in one of the wards at the Red Cross Annexe military hospital in Farnham Road.

A similar welcome was given to a group of about fifty men from the 1/5th Battalion of The Queen's who arrived in Guildford from Mesopotamia on the morning of Saturday, 3 May 1919. They too received a very warm welcome as they marched up the High Street before retiring to Bretts' restaurant (where WHSmith is today) for what was described as 'a substantial meat breakfast'.

Another small group arrived home on Monday, 17 May 1919, somewhat to the surprise of the town's 'welcome home committee'. However, they quickly responded and among the men they welcomed were one officer and eight other ranks that had gone to France at the very start of the war. They too were treated to a meal at Bretts' restaurant.

Nearly a year after hostilities had ceased, and after the rest of the 1/5th Battalion of The Queen's had come home, a reunion was held at the Drill Hall in Sandfield Terrace. About 1,000 men sat down to dinner after they had taken part in a parade at the Sports Ground in Woodbridge Road and attended a service at Holy Trinity church.

Row upon row of wooden huts at Witley Camp, on heathland about 9 miles from Guildford.

But not everything was peace and harmony, as there were 30,000 disgruntled soldiers camped just a few miles from Guildford. They too were waiting to go back to their homes – on the other side of the Atlantic in Canada. Trips to Guildford in their spare time and their drinking in the town's pubs led to friction between the Canadians and the locals.

Witley Camp was established in 1915 on the heaths of Witley and Rodborough Commons. Today, the thick wooded area on either side of the A3 between the Milford and Thursley junctions gives no indication of the size of the sprawling camp that was once there. It consisted of row upon row of wooden huts and a number of ancillary buildings that even included a veterinary hospital. There was also a post office, YMCA huts and chapels and, beside the main road, civilian-run shops, two banks, and a theatre/cinema – together known as 'Tin Town'.

Throughout the war, British and Canadian soldiers passed through the camp, usually spending about six weeks there on training before being deployed to other camps or to the front. Life at the camp was probably no different to similar ones throughout Britain at the time. Some men suffered from illness, and the *Surrey Times* reported in 1915 that at Witley Camp there had been cases of spotted fever and scarlet fever, with the men being removed to a hospital in Aldershot.

The camp also employed civilians as carpenters and labourers. It was noticed that items belonging to the military were being stolen, and so in 1915, as they clocked off and were walking out of the camp, forty-seven of them were arrested by officers of the Surrey Constabulary and Military Police. Crimes in the camp committed by soldiers and civilians alike was commonplace. It ranged from drunkenness, shop breaking, peddling and hawking to assault, loitering and prostitution.

By 1919, with men having returned home to Guildford from the war and Canadians from Witley Camp pouring into the town for recreation and acquainting themselves with local girls, tension was rising. On one particular Saturday night, a large group of demobilised men and soldiers of The Queen's Regiment assembled outside a hall where a dance was taking place. As the Canadians left, with girls on their arms, they were attacked. A fight followed and a corporal and a driver were injured. Military and civil police later dispersed the crowd. The following night, a British soldier pushed a Canadian through a window. The presence of mounted police officers prevented further disorder until 11 p.m., when there were more scuffles. The mounted police charged and the crowd broke up.

Items recovered by the author from a rubbish tip used by Witley Camp. Shown are a range of bottles, cutlery, mugs, a toothbrush, tobacco pipe, buttons, badges and even a fragment of a harmonica!

A few nights later, about 100 Canadians came into Guildford. From the railway station, they made their way to the High Street, where they lined up. They then ran up the hill, shouting, 'What's the matter with Canada?' Mounted police charged and the Canadians scattered.

Canadian soldiers were then banned from the town, but by June 1919, they were getting extremely restless back at Witley Camp. Trouble was brewing. However, on the afternoon of Saturday, 14 June at Witley parish church, Miss Dorothy Alice Reed, elder daughter of Mr and Mrs Charles Reed of Wormley, married Lieutenant James Archibald McPhail MM, 4th Battalion 3rd Canadian Reserve. The report in the following week's *Surrey Advertiser* stated that the 'bride wore a dress of white satin with a wreath of orange blossom, and veil of embroidered net – lent for the occasion by a friend in Ireland – and carried a sheaf of

A typical silk wedding dress of the First World War period.

beautiful white flowers. She was attended by four bridesmaids. Lieutenant Lang was best man and Sergeant W.L. Farman, a well-known Canadian organist, presided at the organ. The happy couple later left for London, en route to North Wales'.

Lieutenant McPhail and his bride were fortunate to be away from Witley, as later that day saw the first of two nights of rioting with the shops and theatre at 'Tin Town' burned to the ground. The *Surrey Advertiser* reported:

On both nights the wildest pandemonium prevailed amongst the rioters, and at times there were ugly situations, especially when an armed guard put in an appearance on Sunday night ... The military authorities were powerless to stop the riotous behaviour of the troops, many of whom carried short thick sticks, but owing to the dense crowd of soldiers and the wild confusion it was impossible to see or hear what was occurring except at the actual spot where one happened to be standing. Above the din and noise of the shouting rifle or revolver shots occasionally rang out, but these came from parts of the camp some considerable distance from the scene of the rioting, and are said to have been fired by excited soldiers in a spirit of bravado rather than with any serious intention.

An armed guard from nearby Bramshott Camp arrived in a motor lorry, only to have sticks, stones and other missiles hurled at it, and the rioters made a rush for it. On the Saturday night, the camp's own fire brigade, assisted by fireman and engine from Godalming, did their best to stop the fire engulfing 'Tin Town' from spreading to the rest of the camp. The press report added:

Their arrival at the scene was signalised by ironical cheers and shouts by the turbulent troops, one section declaring that if the engine had belonged to the Guildford Brigade, it would have been consigned to the flames, and never have returned to the town, which had been placed out of bounds to Canadians.

The shops and buildings of 'Tin Town' that were beside the camp on what is now the A3.

Further describing the scenes, the newspaper went on:

> The noise created by the rioters was almost indescribable, wild shrieking and shouting being mingled with a babble of voices, while here and there mouth-organs, and in one place a piano, were being played. A large body of rioters who had got completely out of hand marched to the guardrooms and secured the release of a number of prisoners. Another crowd proceeded to what is known as the Special Hospital, broke down the wire fencing encircling it, and it is stated, rolled casks of beer into it … On Sunday morning Tin Town presented the appearance of a heap of ruins. The theatre, Salvation Army hut, and the shops involved had been reduced to ashes, and the other shops ransacked and badly broken about. Doors, windows and other woodwork wrenched from the buildings and thrown into the roadway on Saturday night were scattered everywhere on either side of the Portsmouth Road. Against the ruins of the theatre was exhibited the notice 'Closed for repairs'.

The report also told of the destruction of the buildings:

> Something like twenty buildings were burnt or broken up. The majority of them used by Godalming, Milford and Aldershot tradesmen, were built of wood and galvanised iron. The bulk of them bordered the western side of the

Portsmouth Road at the top of Rodborough Hill, and a few were situated on the opposite side of the road at the Thursley end of the camp. The garrison theatre under the management of the NACB [Navy Army Catering Board] was a popular place of amusement with the troops.

The *Advertiser* reporter was Frederick Milton, who lived at Godalming, and who had served with the forces during the war. He later told an inquiry and court hearing into the riot:

> I arrived at the camp shortly after 10 o'clock and remained there after the disturbance had died down about 11.30 p.m. I estimate the number of soldiers to be about 20,000. The military police were powerless to stop the disturbance. There seemed to be a great deal of indiscriminate firing.

At the same hearing, local Witley police sergeant Frederick Hornett said that he became aware of the Saturday night riot 'through seeing the glare of the fire' and went to the camp as a sightseer in plain clothes and not on official duty. He recalled: 'A Canadian officer saw me, and said to me: "For God's sake clear out of this – it is more than your life is worth to be seen here."'

'Tin Town' after it was looted and torched by Canadian soldiers.

He added that he saw four or five lorries of military police that he believed came from Aldershot, to assist in quelling the riot. In fact, this was not the first disturbance at the camp after the war. There had been one on Armistice Day itself and Hornett recalled that there had been another in February 1919. In giving his opinion for the cause of the riots, he said:

> The disturbance in both February and June were directed against the civilian premises in the camp. In February they were looted and damaged, in June they were totally destroyed by fire. The military portions of the camp were not touched. It was common talk in the camp and outside that the reason for this was that the soldiers were incensed against the shopkeepers for having charged them excessive prices, especially after the towns of Guildford and Godalming had been placed out of bounds, and that they were determined to get even with them. Subsequently, the soldiers complained of the delay in their return to Canada.

GERMAN PRISONERS AT LANGTON PRIORY
Langton Priory, off Portsmouth Road, was used to billet forty German prisoners of war in 1918. Believed to have been mainly officers, they worked on local farms. Some left their mark by scratching their names in the house's lead window frames.

During the morning of Sunday, 15 June, after the riots of the night before, General Sir W. Turner toured the camp with its commandant, General A.H. Bell. Turner denounced the action of the rowdy element that was responsible for the outbreak in very vigorous terms. According to him, he and everyone else were anxious to get back to Canada, but they must all exercise a little patience. He announced that ships would be ready in two weeks' time, but strikes at Southampton and elsewhere had held up shipping. On the Monday after the second night of rioting, the military authorities arrested a number of men who were regarded as ringleaders in the disturbance. Later that day, accompanied by a strong escort, they were removed from the camp handcuffed.

The official end of the Great War came on 28 June 1919, with the signing of the Treaty of Versailles. The High Sheriff of Surrey, Mr J.H. Bridges, read the proclamation of peace from the balcony

NAVAL OFFICER'S DEATH FROM SPANISH FLU

The influenza pandemic of 1918 may have killed up to 100 million people worldwide. One who succumbed in Guildford was Royal Navy Lieutenant Harold Mowll. He died at the Royal Surrey County Hospital in October of that year and was buried at Stoughton Cemetery with full military honours.

of Guildford's Guildhall on the morning of 2 July, at which point the national anthem was sung, followed by loud cheers for King George V. Town crier Albany Peters rang a new bell presented to him courtesy of the magazine *John Bull*, in recognition of his assistance with fundraising during the war and his duties at the town's recruiting marches in 1914 and 1915.

Sunday, 6 July saw services of thanksgiving for the terms of peace held in Guildford's churches and chapels. In addition, a service of all denominations that was attended by several thousand people was held in the Great Quarry, off Shalford Road. The local Salvation Army band led the singing.

There was a public holiday on Saturday, 9 July to celebrate the peace and Guildford responded with a number of civic and public events. These were organised to take into account those still mourning the loss of loved ones and were therefore of a sombre nature rather than of a cheerful celebration. People did display plenty of flags for what was called Peace Day, though, and the church bells rang out. The mayoress (Mrs Tavener) was presented with an addition to the borough's regalia in the form of a new badge and chain, being a smaller replica of that worn by the mayor. It was paid for by the Guildford Chamber of Trade to commemorate the peace treaty and as a tribute to women for the vital part they had played in the Allies winning

Civic dignitaries on the balcony of the Guildhall for the reading of the official proclamation of peace on 2 July 1919.

the war. Following the planting of an oak sapling in the Castle Grounds, known as the Peace Oak, the mayor and mayoress returned to the Guildhall. There the High Steward of Surrey, Sir Harry Waechter, presented them and other members of the council with a large silver cup to mark the occasion of peace. Sir Harry also presented a scholarship of £50 to Guildford's Royal Grammar School, along with £3,000 worth of war bonds to pay for an annual scholarship.

The planting of a peace tree by the mayoress, Mrs Tavener, in the Castle Grounds on Saturday, 9 July 1919. The tree survived until it was felled in 1970.

During the afternoon, Stoke Park was the venue for sports and games attended by nearly 4,000 children. The town saw a procession of decorated vehicles and, in the evening, a torchlight procession from North Street to the Sports Ground, where there was a fireworks display. In the weeks following 'Peace Day', the mayor and mayoress distributed Borough of Guildford peace medals, made of a light metal, to local schoolchildren.

Next, Guildford began to focus on the rightful way to remember its war dead. At the same time, thoughts were being gathered for other smaller memorials – in villages, schools and workplaces.

Borough of Guildford's Peace Celebration commemorative medal.

The North Street Tank

A rather strange gift presented to Guildford in recognition of its efforts in raising money through war savings schemes was a tank that had seen action on the Western Front.

Things did not bode well for its residency from the moment it arrived by rail at London Road station. On 27 August 1919, the mayor and his councillors assembled in North Street, where the tank was to be driven to for the official handover. But at the railway station the tank would not start, despite all the efforts made by the officer in charge. The mayor and his entourage then hastily made their way to the stricken vehicle for the formal presentation.

Two days later, the tank was fitted with a new magneto, whereupon its engine burst into life. It then slowly made its way down the High Street to the bottom of North Street. Its resting place was at the junction with Friary Street – near today's open space known as the Rotunda.

There was an unfortunate incident during its short journey as one of the town councillors, Mr W.F. Swayne, was having a look inside the tank when it moved off. He was stuck inside the confined space the crew worked in, and witnessed first-hand the ear-shattering noise made by the tank, the sheer heat from its engine and petrol fumes. It was said that when he finally climbed out the tank after it had come to rest, he said he had been nearly roasted.

Soon people were complaining that the presence of this beast, that looked exactly as it had when it left the battlefield, was rekindling memories of the war that many were trying to forget. Public pressure finally won over any who wanted it to remain, and in 1923 it was cut up for scrap and all traces of it removed.

The tank presented to Guildford on its way to the junction of North Street and Friary Street.

Postscript

Legacy

The long, hard slog that so many had endured throughout the war unfortunately continued after peace had been secured. Victory celebrations had been short lived, and while everyone was hoping for a better future, life in Britain for the majority of its population was not going to get much better.

Although in June 1918, all men over the age of 21 and women over the age of 30 were given the vote for the first time, Britain had been left heavily in debt as a result of the war. Soon, workers' strikes were commonplace and in 1921 unemployment soared to 11.3 per cent. Working women were also finding that they were being forced to give up their jobs to the returning servicemen.

One thing that was not going to go away were the nightmares and flashbacks suffered by those who had taken part in the bloodshed on the battlefield and who had witnessed all kinds of horrific scenes. And above all, there were the everlasting thoughts of families who had lost loved ones.

Addison Road in Charlotteville lost ten of its young men to active service, while from the comparatively small Falcon Road, off York Road, eleven men did not return. Mr and Mrs Bannister of Pannels Terrace, off Chertsey Street, lost two sons: Lance Corporal E. Bannister, of the Royal Dublin Fusiliers, who died in France in June 1917 and Private B. Bannister, of the York and Lancaster Regiment, who died of illness in Leeds in 1919. Mr H. Briant of 4 South Road, Stoughton, lost sons Sergeant C.E. Briant, of the Dorset Regiment, who died of wounds in

October 1917 and Private A. Briant, of the London Regiment, who died in Egypt in March 1918. Mentioned in an earlier chapter are the two Parsons brothers who died within a short time of each other in 1916, and the three men of the Collier family from Springfield Road. Harry and Lucy Ruffell of 49 Walnut Tree Close also lost three sons: Corporal A. Ruffell, of the Rifle Brigade, died of wounds in France in May 1915; Corporal Ernie Ruffell, of The Queen's, is believed to have died in Palestine in December 1917; and Lance Corporal W. Ruffell, of the Worcestershire Regiment, died in France in August 1916.

The Wallingtons of 40 Guildford Park Road were another family with three sons who did not return: Private F.J. Wallington, Northamptonshire Regiment, died in France in July 1916; Private W.J. Wallington of The Queen's died in France in September 1915; and Private A.H. Wallington, of the East Yorkshire Regiment, died in France in 1918.

There were of course people well known to many in Guildford who mourned the loss of sons serving overseas. Widow Clara Dean was the landlady of the Two Brewers pub in Castle Street (now the Keep). Her fourth son, Private Elliot James Dean, was a regular soldier with the Northampton Regiment and at the start of the war, his battalion was stationed in Alexandra, Egypt. He returned once to Guildford in 1914 on forty-eight hours' leave. On 5 November, however, he went with his regiment to France and by 20 November had died of wounds.

Lieutenant Reginald Henry Lutwidge Dodgson, of the Royal Defence Corps, died from illness in Cardiff in May 1918. He was the son of Wilfred and Alice Dodgson, who lived at the Chestnuts in Castle Hill. Wilfred (died 1914) was the brother of the Revd Charles Lutwidge Dodgson, better known as Lewis Carroll, the author of *Alice's Adventures in Wonderland* and *Through the Looking-Glass*. The Dodgson's connection with the Chestnuts began when the reverend leased it in 1868 as a home for his younger brothers and sisters after the death of their father.

As early as February 1919, discussions took place for a suitable memorial to commemorate the town's war dead. A public meeting was held and a committee formed to look for a suitable

The unveiling and dedication of Guildford's war memorial in the Castle Grounds on Sunday, 6 November 1921.

site and to choose a design. The problem was that there wasn't much money around to spend. The committee agreed on a budget of £1,500, with £25 to the person who came up with the best design. The noted architect Sir Edwin Lutyens agreed to judge the entries and the one he chose, by a Mr Denning of Bristol, was not much thought of by the memorial committee. There was a further hitch as only £600 had been raised to pay for it. The committee then appealed to local architects to submit designs, with the one by Frederick Hodgson deemed suitable and affordable.

Lutyens was also a member of those tasked with finding a site for the memorial and it was with his approval that a position just inside the Castle Grounds in front of the bowling green was decided upon. It was unveiled and dedicated on Sunday, 6 November 1921. Approximately 5,000 people packed into the Castle Grounds to witness the event. A civic procession walked from the Guildhall to the Castle Grounds led by the Guildford and District Military Band, playing Chopin's 'Funeral March'. The Bishop of Winchester, Dr E.S. Talbot, and clergy from several Guildford churches conducted the service of dedication, with Lieutenant General Sir Edmund Elles performing the unveiling by releasing flags that had covered the memorial.

The memorial takes the form of a Doric-style colonnade made of limestone that is raised on three steps with urns that symbolise ashes. The names of the war dead are inscribed on Portland stone panels. It was hoped that these would be of brass, but there were insufficient funds at the time.

The names that appear on the roll of honour were complied by the then editor of the *Surrey Advertiser*, William Oakley, and architect Harvey Lunn, both of whom were members of the war memorial committee. Their list numbered some 492 men, all of whose names, regimental details and date of death were included

The editor of the Surrey Advertiser *at the time of the First World War, William Oakley, helped compile the names for Guildford's roll of honour.*

on the memorial. However, two names had to be removed when it was discovered that they hadn't died at all! Between the names Collyer and Cook, the name of Comber has been chiselled out. It is believed that he was wounded on the battlefield, taken prisoner and subsequently transferred to a hospital in eastern Germany. He remained there until he recovered, by which time the war had been over for six months. His family had been told that he was 'missing, presumed dead', so when the roll of honour was compiled soon after the Armistice, his name was naturally added. It is likely that the error had not been discovered when the

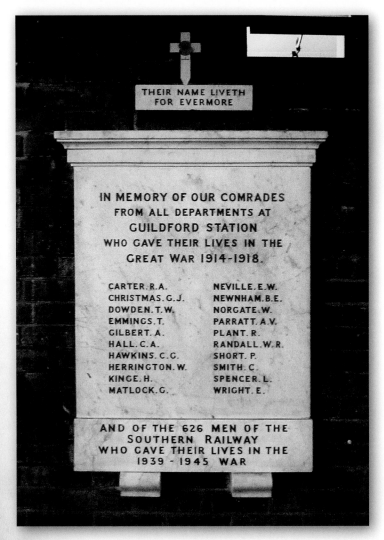

IN MEMORY OF OUR COMRADES
FROM ALL DEPARTMENTS AT
GUILDFORD STATION
WHO GAVE THEIR LIVES IN THE
GREAT WAR 1914-1918.

CARTER. R.A.	NEVILLE. E.W.
CHRISTMAS. G.J.	NEWNHAM. B.E.
DOWDEN. T.W.	NORGATE. W.
EMMINGS. T.	PARRATT. A.V.
GILBERT. A.	PLANT. R.
HALL. C.A.	RANDALL. W.R.
HAWKINS. C.G.	SHORT. P.
HERRINGTON. W.	SMITH. C.
KINGE. H.	SPENCER. L.
MATLOCK. G.	WRIGHT. E.

AND OF THE 626 MEN OF THE
SOUTHERN RAILWAY
WHO GAVE THEIR LIVES IN THE
1939 - 1945 WAR

A memorial plaque at Guildford railway station names those who worked from there and who died on active service between 1914 and 1918.

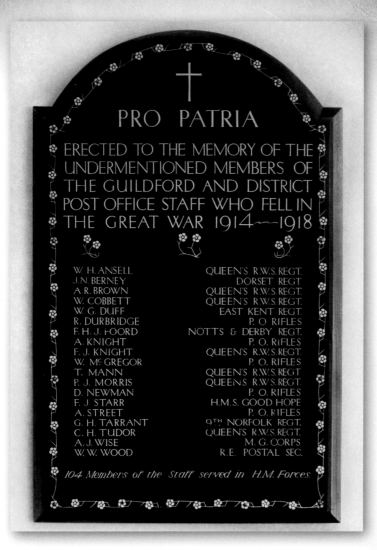

*Men from Guildford
and district killed in
the First World War
who worked for
Royal Mail.*

PRO PATRIA	
ERECTED TO THE MEMORY OF THE UNDERMENTIONED MEMBERS OF THE GUILDFORD AND DISTRICT POST OFFICE STAFF WHO FELL IN THE GREAT WAR 1914—1918	
W. H. ANSELL	QUEEN'S R.W.S. REGT.
J. N. BERNEY	DORSET REGT.
A. R. BROWN	QUEEN'S R.W.S. REGT.
W. COBBETT	QUEEN'S R.W.S. REGT.
W. G. DUFF	EAST KENT REGT.
R. DURBRIDGE	P. O. RIFLES
F. H. J. FOORD	NOTTS & DERBY REGT.
A. KNIGHT	P. O. RIFLES
F. J. KNIGHT	QUEEN'S R.W.S. REGT.
W. McGREGOR	P. O. RIFLES
T. MANN	QUEEN'S R.W.S. REGT.
P. J. MORRIS	QUEENS R.W.S. REGT.
D. NEWMAN	P. O. RIFLES
F. J. STARR	H.M.S. GOOD HOPE
A. STREET	P. O. RIFLES
G. H. TARRANT	9TH NORFOLK REGT.
C. H. TUDOR	QUEEN'S R.W.S. REGT.
A. J. WISE	M. G. CORPS
W. W. WOOD	R.E. POSTAL SEC.
104 Members of the Staff served in H.M. Forces	

memorial was unveiled two years later. The other gap is between the names Jelly and Jewsbury, but whose name this is the author does not know.

Villages and hamlets throughout Britain also erected memorials to men from those communities, even though their names may already have appeared on larger town and city memorials. These smaller memorials are found in a range of different locations, from village greens to churchyards. In today's borough of Guildford, war memorials can be found in most of its villages, from Ash in the west (113 names) to Effingham in the east (100 names).

The memorial to The Queen's (Royal West Surrey) Regiment in Holy Trinity church, Guildford.

Further memorials were erected in some schools as a permanent reminder of former pupils who had given their lives, and also at places where men worked, as well as on plaques inside churches (as at St Mary's in Worplesdon). At Guildford's Royal Grammar School, the names of fifty-eight of its 'old boys' are on its First World War memorial plaque, while a memorial plaque at Guildford railway station lists twenty men who worked at or from the station, although their home addresses may not have been in Guildford.

The Royal Mail sorting office in Woodbridge Meadows has a memorial on display with the names of nineteen Guildford and district postmen who made the supreme sacrifice. It contains a reminder that 'this memorial may not be removed without the express permission of Royal Mail'.

Holy Trinity Church in Guildford High Street features the First World War memorial to The Queen's (Royal West Surrey) Regiment. The names of 8,000 men of all ranks who fell in the war are commemorated in a book of remembrance. It was unveiled and dedicated on 4 June 1921.

Intriguingly, a memorial on the Guildford borough boundary with Woking at Fox Corner, Worplesdon, has no names on it at all. It reads: 'Lest we forget. To the glory of God and in honoured memory of those of our forces who passed this spot and who gave their lives for their country in the Great War 1914–1918.' The site of this wayside memorial would certainly have seen a good deal of troop movements, being so close to Pirbright Camp.

Memorials to a single serviceman were also erected, and Guildford can claim to have one of these. It originally took the form of a Calvary cross and was unveiled outside St Nicolas' church at the foot of the High Street on 12 April 1919. In 1914, the Reverend Erasmus Austin Ommanney had returned to the church for the second time as a curate, having previously served as a commander in the Royal Navy. His son, Second Lieutenant Alfred Ommanney (The Buffs) East Kent Regiment, was killed during the Battle of the Somme. The cross with a plinth containing an inscription was erected in his memory, but soon there was a good deal of opposition from local people who did not approve of the nature of the memorial. The cross was later removed, but the plinth and inscription can still be seen.

In recent years there has been a growing interest in many of the war memorials in the borough of Guildford and the names they contain. Merrow's memorial in the churchyard of the parish church of St John the Evangelist underwent an £18,000 restoration, followed by an ecumenical rededication service on 12 May 2002. The project, led by local resident Tony Neale, also included much new research into the men named on it. The author assisted Mr Neale in a small way by helping to trace the date of its original unveiling in 1920 as reported in the *Surrey Advertiser*. Today the church displays a leather-bound book of remembrance that not only has the names of those listed on the memorial, but details of their service records, date of death, place of burial if known, photographs and so on. Copies of the book were also presented to the Surrey History Centre and Guildford Museum.

Within the parish of Holy Trinity in Guildford, there is a war memorial cross in front of the Addison Court flats in Addison Road that contains the names of twenty-five men from Charlotteville who died in the First World War and a further seven from the Second World War. St Luke's chapel, a 'tin-tabernacle' building of green corrugated iron, once stood here. The memorial is not on its original site, and research by local resident Ian Nicholls has uncovered a wealth of details about it and information of the men named and this can be found on his excellent website (details in bibliography). It is now the focus of a service of remembrance each year on the Saturday afternoon before Remembrance Sunday. A reception is usually held afterwards at which, while enjoying refreshments, people can view a number of display panels relating to the war memorial and the local history of Charlotteville.

Laying wreaths at the war memorial in Addison Road, Charlotteville.

The Stoke-next-Guildford war memorial in its original position in the churchyard opposite St John's church.

At least one other Guildford war memorial has been moved. The monument commemorating the men from Stoke-next-Guildford who lost their lives during warfare was originally sited within the churchyard opposite St John's church in Stoke Road, but it can now be seen on the opposite side of the road near the junction with Lido Road.

St Luke's church in Burpham contains the names of eighteen servicemen who gave their lives during the Great War. Recent interest in who they were and where they lived is the subject of ongoing research by local people (details in bibliography).

Services of remembrance for men of the armed forces who died in the First World War began soon after the end of hostilities. For many years, men of the Old Contemptible's Association, veterans who had been part of the British Expeditionary Force who had gone to France in 1914, paraded through Guildford on or around St George's Day (23 April). They continued this tradition until all had 'grown old'.

In recognition of the sacrifice made by so many, Britain's war memorials, large or small, ornate or simple (many also containing names of those who died in the Second World War), continue to be the focus for acts of remembrance each

Led by their president, Brigadier George Rupell VC CB (wearing the bowler hat), men of the Guildford branch of the Old Contemptibles' Association march down the High Street in the late 1940s during their annual parade. They were veterans who had been part of the 1914 British Expeditionary Force in France.

year, either on Armistice Day (11 November) or Remembrance Sunday. Thankfully, the public's support for these moving services has increased in recent years. Whether it is because we live in times where there is still conflict in the world and in which British forces are inevitably involved, or because the interest in the history of warfare (in particular the Great War) remains strong with new analysis and opinions expressed, or the fact that an ever increasing number of people are enjoying the fascination of family and local history, it matters not. What does matter is that 'at the going down of the sun and in the morning, we will remember them'.

BIBLIOGRAPHY AND SOURCES

Books

Crocker, Glenys, *Chilworth Gunpowder* (Surrey Industrial History Group, 1984)

McNab, Chris, *The World War I Story* (The History Press, 2011)

Mercer, Sarah, *St John Ambulance in Guildford: The First 50 Years* (self-published, 2004)

Oakley, W.H., *Guildford In The Great War* (Billing & Sons Ltd, 1934)

Parker, Eric, *Surrey* (Robert Hale Ltd, 1947)

Wylly, Colonel H.C., *History of The Queen's (Royal West Surrey) Regiment in the Great War* (Gale & Polden Ltd, 1925; The Naval & Military Press Ltd, 2003).

Memoirs

Powell, Elizabeth Beatrice, *Piccard's Rough 1914–19: A Convalescent Hospital* (1938)

Websites

Ahoy – Mac's Web Log:
   http://ahoy.tk-jk.net/macslog/
   ShotatDawnWW1ArmyExecutio.html

Burpham 'We Will Remember Them' war memorial project:
   www.burpham1914.org.uk/

Charlotteville war memorial:
   www.users.waitrose.com/~iannicholls/Local-History.html

Metrological Office:
www.metoffice.gov.uk/archive/monthly-weather-report-1910s
Surrey Infantry Museum:
www.queensroyalsurreys.org.uk/index.shtml
The Long, Long Trail:
www.1914-1918.net/recruitment.htm

Great War Britain:
The First World War at Home

Luci Gosling

After the declaration of war in 1914, the conflict dominated civilian life for the next four years. Magazines quickly adapted without losing their gossipy essence: fashion jostled for position with items on patriotic fundraising, and court presentations were replaced by notes on nursing. The result is a fascinating, amusing and uniquely feminine perspective of life on the home front.

978 0 7524 9188 2

The First World War in 100 Objects

Peter Doyle

Objects allow us to understand the experience of men and women during the First World War. This book focuses on weapons like the machine gun and vehicles such as the tank that transformed the battlefield and German submarines that stalked shipping across the seas, as well as everyday objects transformed by the harsh realities of war. Through these incredible artefacts, Peter Doyle tells the story of the First World War in a whole new light.

978 0 7524 8811 0

Visit our website and discover many other First World War books.

www.thehistorypress.co.uk/first-world-war

The
History
Press